HEALING THE SOUL

Unexpected Stories of Courage, Hope, and the Power of Mind

HEALING THE SOUL

Unexpected Stories of Courage, Hope, and the Power of Mind

Bhupendra O. Khatri, MD

Henschel
HAUS
Milwaukee, Wisconsin

Published by
HenschelHAUS Publishing, Inc.
2625 S. Greeley St. Suite 201
Milwaukee, WI 53207
www.henschelHAUSbooks.com

ISBN: 978-1-59598-344-2
E-ISBN: 978-1-59598-345-9

Library of Congress Control Number: 2014949729

Publisher's Cataloging-In-Publication Data
(Prepared by The Donohue Group, Inc.)
Khatri, Bhupendra O.
Healing the soul : unexpected stories of courage, hope, and the power of
mind / Bhupendra O. Khatri, MD.

pages : illustrations ; cm

Includes index.
Issued also as an ebook.
ISBN: 978-1-59598-344-2

1. Mental healing. 2. Patients--Psychology. 3. Mind and body. 4. Attitude
(Psychology) 5. Medicine--Practice--21st century. I. Title.

RZ400 .K43 2014
615.8528   2014949729

Cover design: Peggy Nehmen, N-KCreative.com
Editor: Bobbi Linkemer, www.writeanonfictionbook.com
Index: Galen Schroeder, www.dakotaindexing.com

*A portion of the proceeds from the sale of this book
shall be donated to MS research.*

PRAISE FOR *HEALING THE SOUL*

Healing the Soul is a precious gift not only to those who bear the burden of life-altering illness, but especially to physicians striving to truly care for such persons in this modern era of too much technology and too little time. Spending that time with and for the patients for whom one is privileged to care— laying hands on the patient and not the computer; listening instead of lecturing; truly caring for the human being whose trust you have been given, not earned—all such actions bring immeasurable reward, thoughtfully and meaningfully described by Dr. Khatri. Read what he has written, and give thanks for the reward you will be given, in return!

—Michael McQuillen MD,
neurologist, ethicist, and teacher, Stanford University (retired)

- - - - - - - - - - - -

In his book, *Healing the Soul: Unexpected Stories of Courage, Hope, and the Power of Mind*, Bhupendra Khatri presents a series of compelling stories that speak to the power of positive thinking and, indeed, the power of the mind. Each and every one of us can accomplish so much more and overcome seemingly insurmountable obstacles by simply keeping a positive 'can do' attitude. Dr. Khatri's book provides testimony to this in an extraordinarily eloquent manner. Simply stated, his book is a must-read for those who doubt themselves in times of stress or when under siege by illness or other obstacles that life presents.

—Edward C. Benzel, MD,
Chairman of the Cleveland Clinic Spine Institute
Chairman, Neurosurgery, Cleveland Clinic

- - - - - - - - - - - -

Healing the Soul hit me in the gut and made me cry! It touched my soul! A very powerful book of courage, determination, and the power of the positive thinking. It will inspire you to conquer your own mind and eventually help you succeed in being strong or whatever you desire to be. A must read for those who want to be real men!

—Silas Young , an American professional wrestler,
Ring Of Honor Wrestling, best known as
"The Last Real Man In Professional Wrestling"

- - - - - - - - - - - -

I have known Dr. Khatri for more than three decades. He is well known as a leading neurologist for the care of people who have multiple sclerosis. The book is based on his experiences in caring for patients during his professional career. The book should be of interest to those diagnosed with multiple sclerosis and their families, as well as health professionals.

Dr. Khatri also shares his observations on the politics of healthcare and the increasing demands on physicians' time by the government regulations and insurance companies, which cut into the time physicians can devote to the care of the sick. He also delves into the healing effects of positive thinking and spirituality.

The book should appeal to anyone interested in learning more about experiences and beliefs of a dedicated physician who has devoted his life to the care of patients with multiple sclerosis, a potentially disabling disease that remains an enigma for which there is no known cause or cure.

—Mahendr S. Kochar MD, MACP
Professor and Associate Dean, University of California, Riverside School of
Medicine, author of Textbook of
Medicine & Kochar's Clinical Medicine for Students

- - - - - - - - - - - -

Healing the Soul touched my heart while stimulating my intellect. Dr. Khatri weaves together inspiring true stories of his patients, extolling the resiliency of the human spirit and the power of the mind-body connection. This unique blend of the spiritual and medical is a must-read for every patient, doctor, and indeed anyone wanting to explore the mystery of the human condition.

—Jeffrey Small,
bestselling author of The Breath of God and The Jericho Deception

Dr. Khatri points out that the mind is a powerful instrument and can potentially be utilized in healing. He teaches us that we must pay attention to the power of the mind and attempt to direct it toward improving quality of life or allow for comfort in the passing of life. The stories of his patients bring tears to our eyes showing that positive attitude has the potential to change lives of people with chronic diseases. A powerful book and a must read for patients and clinicians, alike.

Randall T. Schapiro, M.D., FAAN
President, The Schapiro Multiple Sclerosis Advisory Group
Clinical Professor of Neurology (Retired)
University of Minnesota
Author of the bestselling book,
Managing the Symptoms of Multiple Sclerosis

- - - - - - - - - - -

In this unique collection of stories, Dr. Khatri, a superb clinician and humanist, illustrates many of the important issues confronting patients and their health care providers. Dr. Khatri utilizes the time-honored technique elucidating the salient point of every chapter with a case history. His descriptions reveal the lessons this warm, caring, and thoughtful physician has learned from his patients. Some of the of the topics covered, such as the mind-body relationship and the importance of living life to the fullest in light of its short and capricious nature, are universal and timeless. Others, such as, the impact of the electronic health records on the doctor-patient relationship, are more contemporary. This anthology that reflects on the human condition through illness is both wonderfully engaging and educational.

—Joseph R. Berger, M.D.
Professor of Neurology
Chief, Multiple Sclerosis Division
Perelman School of Medicine
University of Pennsylvania

- - - - - - - - - - -

My congratulations to Dr. Khatri for allowing us to hear the important voices of these brave fighters who deal with the difficult, debilitating disease of MS. It is through their stories that we can communicate hope to our own patients and those who care for them. I also commend Dr. Khatri for his clear-eyed analysis of EHR—its positive contributions to the field of medicine and its negative consequences to patient care.

Omar Khan, MD
Professor & Chair, Department of Neurology, Wayne State University
School of Medicine , Neurologist-in-Chief, The Detroit Medical Center Associate
Chief Medical Officer, Wayne State University Physicians
Group Director, The Sastry Foundation
Advanced Imaging Laboratory Director,
Multiple Sclerosis Center for Research and Treatment
Wayne State University School of Medicine

- - - - - - - - - -

Dr. Bhupendra Khatri's book *Healing The Soul* has left a deep and lasting impression on me. The very first story touched my heart and set the tone for the rest of the book. I could not resist sitting up and reading it cover to cover. This book is especially relevant in today's practice of medicine, where technology appears to have eclipsed the art of healing. We deal with sick persons—not just diseases—and what the patients expect of their physicians is very well reflected in this book. Touching, real-life accounts of the patients' struggles, their courage in the face of insurmountable odds, and the power of positive thinking are the highlights of this book. Extremely well written, Bhupen. This book is a must for all those involved in patient care.

Bhim Singhal MD,FRCP
Director Neurology, Bombay Hospital Institute of Medical Sciences, Formerly
Professor of Neurology
Grant Medical College and
Sir JJ Group of Hospitals, Mumbai, India

- - - - - - - - - -

The first time I heard Dr. Khatri speak, it became apparent to me that here was a true physician—the type of physician who will never utter, 'There is nothing else I can do for you,' simply because there is always something else he can think of. This book tells the story of Dr. Khatri's connection with his patients, what is there for both the patient and healer in this most sacred relationship.

Regina Berkovich MD
Assistant Professor Neurology,
Keck School of Medicine of USC, Los Angeles, CA

Healing the Soul is a thoughtful, sensitive, emotional, and somewhat philosophical book by Dr. Bhupendra Khatri. It has come out through his intimate relationship with his patients who have a severely disabling disease affecting essentially those in the prime of their lives. He has, through their stories, illustrated several virtues: hope, faith, willpower, spirituality, and the tenacity and selflessness of the caregivers who have sacrificed their own comfort.

Khatri was initiated into medicine and neurology in a large public, government hospital for the poor and underprivileged in Mumbai, India; and it is likely that the sparks of compassion so well revealed in this book must have begun there.

Noshir H. Wadia, MD
FRCP, FNA, FAMS, FASc., DSc. (Hons.), FANA
Erstwhile Honorary Professor of Neurology, Grant Medical College, Mumbai
Consultant Neurologist for Life The J.J. Group of Hospitals, Grant Medical College, Mumbai
Director Emeritus – Department of Neurology, Jaslok Hospital & Research Centre, Mumbai

- - - - - - - - - -

As a clinician and researcher, Dr. Bhupendra Khatri has been a powerful force in the MS movement for decades. All of us who have benefitted from his extraordinary commitment to empowering and caring for those with MS are grateful for his wisdom and generosity. His powerful new book, *Healing the Soul*, is a must read for all who love and care for someone with MS.

Colleen Kalt
President & CEO, National Multiple Sclerosis – Wisconsin Chapter

- - - - - - - - - -

Healing the Soul is a very touching book that brings together the common journey of doctors and patients to find relief and an eventual cure for chronic diseases. The stories provide an open window to better understanding patients' suffering and their hopes, as well as the physician's struggle to ensure patient well-being. "Positive thinking" appears to be the most helpful mediation to reach the ultimate goal. Dr Khatri's devotion to his patients is remarkable, and the stories he presents are proof of the real and difficult role of physicians to diagnose, treat, and support their patients.

The present environment that makes the relationship

between doctor and patient more fragmented can only be overcome with real stories such as those presented in this wonderful book. There is still hope for keeping medicine as an "art of healing" with physicians as Dr Khatri.

Bianca Weinstock-Guttman, MD
Professor of Neurology, SUNY University at Buffalo,
Director Jacobs MS Center for Treatment and Research &
Pediatric MS Center of Excellence
Executive Director NY State MS Consortium

- - - - - - - - - -

After a sudden illness struck eight years ago, I was truly blessed when God led me to my neurologist, Dr. Bhupendra Khatri. His innovative treatments have indeed benefited me greatly, but I have also found that he is a caring, spiritual man who profoundly respects his patients. Dr. Khatri's deeply moving book demonstrates time and again how so many of them have not let terrible pain and crushing disabilities destroy their individual spirit and essential humanity. Their wonderful stories both inspire and humble the reader. One can only pray for the fortitude and strength to meet adversity as well as they have. Dr. Khatri's work, I believe, is yet another manifestation of God's love for all people and represents the true nature of His commandment to love thy neighbor as thyself.

John B. Lundstrom
Curator Emeritus of History
Milwaukee Public Museum
Award-winning author of six books

- - - - - - - - - -

As one who lives with MS, I found *Healing the Soul* a WOW of a read. Dr. Khatri's courageously honest observations of medical science and the mind/body connection are vital ingredients in the healing process. His compassion and patient advocacy are obvious and most appreciated. This book adds certainty to my belief that one's attitude is a big piece of the medical puzzle.

Christine Zapf
Court reporter, MS patient advocate,
outdoor enthusiast, environmental activist

- - - - - - - - - -

Dr. Bhupendra Khatri is a neurologist trained in the scientific tradition who has achieved much in a stellar career. He is esteemed by his colleagues for his meticulous scientific work and has earned that respect. However, as this book clearly shows, he knows that while science must comprise the basis for the effective practice of medicine, there is much more to being a physician than simply having a grasp of scientific facts. He weaves a fascinating tale of the critical role of eye contact, physical touch, compassion, and a sympathetic ear in providing care to his patients. He rails effectively and appropriately against the invasion of the clinical space by administrators and ill-considered regulations that lead to less effective care, poorer outcomes, and low patient satisfaction. This book should be required reading for all physicians in training and I will certainly give a copy to my daughter as she embarks on her medical career. Thank you, Bhupen.

Gareth J Parry, ONZM, MB, ChB, FRACP.
Emeritus Professor of Neurology, University of Minnesota
Consultant Neurologist, Wellington Hospital, New Zealand

- - - - - - - - - - -

Dr. Khatri has written a remarkable and uplifting book with powerful stories from his long clinical practice that contains much clinical wisdom. The reader discovers patients of his who exhibit remarkable courage with the personal strength to maintain hope and purpose in the face of terrible illness, disability, and suffering. Physicians reading the stories can see the indispensability of learning about their patients' lives, hopes, and fears, as well as the profound influence their conversations exert on their patients' attitudes toward their illness and their ability to maintain hope. Dr. Khatri shares personal anecdotes about his life and family, illustrating how spirituality and beliefs are necessary to instil meaning in life. I found these inspiring stories a delight to read.

James L. Bernat, MD
Louis and Ruth Frank Professor of Neuroscience
Professor of Neurology and Medicine
Geisel School of Medicine at Dartmouth

- - - - - - - - - -

Physicians have known for millennia that most of the sick like to be touched; the healthy, less so. Computer programmers and bean counters lack algorithms for touch, for empathy, for caring, for will and determination or lack of same, for hope or despair—in short, for the art of medicine. Dr. Khatri draws attention to the dilemma faced by physicians, forced into an overweening reliance on electronic health records, by means of a series of vignettes drawn from his own experience. The touched—when listened to, watched, and encouraged to unburden themselves of their concerns—provide poignant proof that a true sense of a person and of his attitude will usually emerge. A computer program cannot capture this.

The tales are moving and profound. They make an additional critical point: Mind really matters. Multiple sclerosis is a disease of the nervous system caused by aberrant behavior of the immune system. The two systems continuously interact in both directions. Some of these interactions are subliminal, but some can be influenced, either favorably or unfavorably, by conscious decision. Spirituality and hope, encouraged by a caring physician, can contribute in a major way to health or at least to a positive outcome when health is impaired. The contemplative aspects of this book force the reader to think things through—surely a welcome end result.

Dr. Barry Arnason MD
The James Nelson and Anna Louise Raymond Professor of neurology
The University of Chicago

- - - - - - - - - - - -

I could not put Dr. Khatri's book down. I have never cried so much spontaneously reading a book but yet been inspired about life at the same time. This book should be "required reading" for every medical student and nurse. This book should be put in the hands of every person who is "down" about some condition in their lives. This book puts life in perspective and puts a focus on why we get into healthcare and the core reason we are all alive—helping people.

I have studied everyone from Tony Robbins to Deepak Chopra in my quest to better help people live healthier lives. I can sincerely say that I found your book, Healing the Soul - perhaps one of the most impactful on me.

David D. Erickson, MBA
Owner, Fit4Life

Dr. Khatri's book resembles to some extent a Joycean stream of consciousness, with chapters ranging from "The Power of Positive Thinking"—citing Oprah Winfrey rather than Norman Vincent Peale—to "Brain Dead," where his instincts, background, and training negated the very reasonable assumption that his patient was indeed brain dead by all criteria, leading him to authorize a life-saving organ replacement. The leitmotif of his work seems to me similar to a rather awkward sentence I have used for years to close my *Who's Who* biographies: *To be a physician demands recognition of the intrinsic value and dignity of human life while pursuing the goal of relieving pain and impairment due to disease or injury.*

His fourth chapter, "The Lost Art of Touch," recapitulates what both of us were taught: Essential to the diagnosis is a detailed history and a complete neurologic examination. I cannot make a diagnosis from a check-list. And if I were forced to choose between an exam and a history, my choice—and I suspect that of most older physicians—would be clearly the latter. After all, the history is, or should be, a verbal examination. When I was in training, the senior neurologists paid special attention to it, using but a few tests to confirm what they had already concluded was the problem. I have seen a recent paper recording the demise of the ophthalmoscope in neurology. That is the one essential tool for a neurologic exam; all else can be done with nothing but one's hands and a pin. Neurology was the last specialty board to drop the assessment of actual patients from its certifying exam, which I thought was a huge mistake.

In several chapters, Dr. Khatri shows how the art and skill of neurologic practice are in danger of being markedly degraded by modern advances. Computerized records, extraneous requirements for medically irrelevant record keeping, and responses to demands by insurers and the government have taken up more and more of a physician's time leaving the neurologist with neither time to do the exam he/she wants to do nor the freedom to prescribe the treatment indicated. This is well explicated in his Chapter 16, "Practicing Medicine in the Digital Age," where the physician does not have time even to look at his patient because of the need to complete all the electronic forms that are essential—not for the patient or physician but for the ruling juntas of electronic medicine, whose system is misleadingly referred to as "personalized medicine." Here, though, there may perhaps be light at the end of the tunnel before all our skills are irretrievably lost to later generations of physicians. Not too far in the future, I would hope, there will be a system for automatically recording and digitizing the real-time, spoken words of both patient and physician, which would once again occur face to face.

Dr. Khatri's book should be required reading for all medical students.

John F Kurtzke MD, FACP, FAAN, FANA
Recipient of the Charcot Award and Dystel Prize
Emeritus Professor of Neurology
Georgetown University School of Medicine

TABLE OF CONTENTS

> *Healing the body is a complex process that is influenced by multiple factors, the most important of which is the patient's state of mind. Simply telling a patient to be positive doesn't work; the patient needs to be convinced that recovery will occur. Once the conscious mind accepts this as a fact, the subconscious mind allows healing to take place. Since positive thoughts and energy are powerful therapies that can promote healing, we as physicians, should remember how important attitude—our patients' and our own—is in the healing process.*

> *Few of us depart with everything we ever meant to do wrapped up in a neat package. People who are dying can prolong their own lives for a short time, at least until a strong desire is fulfilled or some sort of closure is achieved. They can also be influenced by their loved ones to live a little longer, even if they are comatose. The subconscious mind never sleeps. An unconscious person's subconscious mind is active and able to perceive and process information through hearing, touch, thoughts, and energy.*

MS is one of the most common causes of progressive neurological disability in young adults, often striking in the prime of their lives. Sharing a diagnosis of MS with the patient is a skill learned over time, but it never gets any easier. Any doctor can write a prescription for a wheelchair, but only patients understand what it really means to give up walking. Yet, they often teach their doctors how to live, with such statements as this one: "You have to dream and live your dreams, even if it is in your imagination."

Healthcare providers are trapped in a system that is overly dependent on technology and leaves little time to spend with patients. The electronic health record (EHR) is supposed to provide efficient, coordinated, high-quality care and produce great cost savings in the future. However, EHR is rapidly eroding the art of practicing medicine, the cost of which will dwarf the benefits and the projected financial savings attributed to it. Somatoform disorders—physical symptoms for which there is no demonstrable organic cause—can be diagnosed by observation, touch, and listening; yet, the art of touch is rapidly being replaced by technology.

Physicians are trained to heal, not to have to fight for what they believe is the right medical therapy for their patients. Yet, insurance companies cite "evidence-based medicine guidelines" to justify denial of treatments, including those approved by the FDA. Non-medical personnel often override the recommendations of treating physicians. Insurance companies are required to provide the cost of the benefit only when the patient survives long enough to re-

ceive it. If the patient dies before receiving the treatment, the insurer pays nothing. There is no meaningful penalty for denying medically necessary treatment.

*rejection, bullying, and even murder. This
makes it a concern of the medical community,
which acknowledges that homosexuality is
neither a health disorder nor a mental illness.
While in some countries it is a crime, in others,
progress is being made.*

*In 1999, Congress passed the Pain Relief
Promotion Act, which encouraged physicians to
treat pain aggressively, even when the treatment might increase the risk of death. Under-
treatment of pain became a punishable crime.
This direct intervention by regulatory agencies,
such as the Joint Commission on Accreditation
of Healthcare Organizations (JCAHO), has led to
catastrophic results, Doctors now write about
three hundred million prescriptions a year for
painkillers. That is enough for every adult
American to be medicated around the clock for a
month, every day; deaths from drug overdose
outnumber gun deaths.*

*According to neuroscientist Dr. Richard David-
son, "The brain is an organ designed to change
in response to experience. Through thought
training," says Dr. Davidson, "you can use the
power of your mind to change the pathways in
your brain." Does that mean that the brain,
consciously or subconsciously, uses information
to push us toward the achievement of our
goals? Research suggests that even a small
amount of positive thinking helps us realize
our goals. Regular meditation has been shown
to sharpen that area of the brain that is
responsible for positive thoughts.*

should be a stepping stone to reach higher ground. When you fail to grow, so does your spirituality. This stagnation can breed religious fanaticism.

While we cannot cure patients of their chronic diseases, we can certainly help them to learn how to positively cope with them and lead happy, fulfilled lives. The emerging field of psychoneuroimmunology (PNI) is the study of the interaction between psychological processes and the nervous and immune systems of the human body. Meditation alone has been shown to have a profound effect, not only in the brain, but also in all of the bodily functions. While 60 percent of happiness is determined by our genetics and environment, the remaining 40 percent is up to us.

Fifty percent of MS patients develop permanent disability within ten years of diagnosis. As time goes by, the burden of caregiving will fall on family members, especially spouses, who are also growing older and experiencing health problems. Unless the parents of disabled children also become disabled, they usually continue to take care of their children at home. The economic impact will be considerable as Baby Boomers age. By 2050, the number of patients with Alzheimer's requiring long-term care will triple. Caregivers tend to suffer physically and emotionally, becoming more prone to depression, physical ailments, and social isolation.

FOREWORD

Perhaps like many people who have been diagnosed with multiple sclerosis, I focused on the words that labeled the disease for me: *chronic, progressive,* and *no cure.* Dr. Khatri's writing begs the direct question: what are we missing in the treatment of a patient's disease? Beyond receiving the benefit of a current therapy and monitoring by an informed medical professional, proper diagnosis should not be the end point of treatment. Dr. Khatri reveals that it may be the individual patient's spirit and resilience, in partnership with the medical professional, that provides the tipping point for a better quality of life and recovery.

Engaging additional mindful techniques to influence a medical outcome begin with acknowledging that we may not possess all of the treatment answers. Each patient's struggle may be as unique as his or her power to overcome life-survival issues. Dr. Khatri shares his experience of how successful treatment must include embracing the patient's fortitude to not be limited to a medically forgone conclusion. He suggests that we shouldn't be limited to current medical protocol and look deeper within the power of the individual's mind to affect their own critical diagnosis. These are real stories recognizing an unquantifiable spark that inspires a care-giver and gives a patient hope against the medical odds.

Fantastic and eye-opening, Dr. Khatri leads a courageous discussion of the mind's power in the course of healing. He shares the gripping and powerful depth of the individual soul through the grace of people experiencing life-threatening medical conditions. In this tapestry of human dignity, woven with the threads of determination and a caring touch, you will discover the often hidden strength to persevere. Dr. Khatri demonstrates that although medical decisions are individually based, it is the human connection throughout life that is the key to live vitally. Through these true stories, discover that even with incapacity there is a calm strength leading people to surpass their own health expectations.

Read this book and you will respect disabling conditions, but not surrender to them. Embrace life.

Jeffrey N. Gingold,
internationally acclaimed author of the award-winning book,
Facing the Cognitive Challenges of Multiple Sclerosis, 2nd Edition and ***Mental Sharpening Stones: Manage the Cognitive Challenges of Multiple Sclerosis***
(both published by Demos Medical Publications).

PREFACE

As we become doctors—and especially after medical school—patients become our teachers. I wrote this book to share the powerful lessons I have learned from my patients and their caregivers. Caring for people with multiple sclerosis, some of whom are still with me, for more than thirty-five years has been a privilege, often uplifting but at times, heart-wrenching.

The practice of medicine in this digital age is highly regulated and changing, and this is adversely affecting the doctor-patient relationship. Physicians are now pulled in so many different directions that it is no wonder that the major complaint of patients is that their doctors do not spend enough time with them. *Healing the Soul* is intended as a reminder that there is no substitute for observation, listening, and touching if you truly want to heal your patients' souls, as well as their bodies.

My patients' stories, which I present here with their permission, are riveting. They inspire us; they teach us; they make us think. They show us the powerful influence the mind has on health and healing. Over the years, I have shared these stories with other healthcare providers, journalists, gym buddies, patients, and writers, all of whom were all so moved and touched by them that they urged me to put them in a book.

While I was compelled to tell these extraordinary stories of courage, hope, and survival, my hope is that they will also inspire those who read them. These stories did not take place in a vacuum. In the background were the often-unseen activities of scientists, family members, insurance companies, politicians, regulatory agencies, clergymen, and activists. All of them provide context for what my patients endured and how they ultimately prevailed.

There is no question that advancements in medical technology are crucial in helping treat disease and alleviate suffering. Nevertheless, it is equally important to remember that a patient is a human being and not a computer screen. Technology's role is to ***augment, not replace***, the art of medicine in healing the soul.

As we enter the digital age of medicine, let us not forget what it really means to put your finger on your patient's pulse!

INTRODUCTION

The current status of multiple sclerosis (MS) is a good-news, bad-news story. The good news is how far we have come in understanding and treating this debilitating disease; the bad news is all that is yet to be done to find a cure.

MS is an unpredictable, often disabling disease of the central nervous system that disrupts the flow of information within the brain and between the brain and the body. It was first identified in 1868 by Jean–Martin Charcot, a French physician who became known as the father of neurology. Almost eighty years later, in 1946, when Sylvia Lawry founded the National MS Society, research on multiple sclerosis was still nonexistent. Diagnosis took years, and there were no proven therapies to slow its progression.

Even today, the cause of MS remains unknown. Scientists are conducting ongoing studies in the fields of immunology, epidemiology, genetics, and infectious diseases in an effort to find the causes and more effective treatments for this elusive condition. The ultimate goal is to find a cure or, better still, eradicate it.

More than 2.3 million people around the world have MS, most diagnosed between the ages of twenty and fifty. Scientists believe that gender, genetics, age, geography, and ethnic background all play some role. While the disease can strike anyone of any race or ethnic background, it is most common in Caucasians of northern European descent and two to three times more often found in women than in men.

The symptoms of MS, which can be devastating, include blurred vision, loss of balance, poor coordination, slurred speech, tremors, numbness, extreme fatigue, problems with memory and concentration, paralysis, and blindness. For some, these symptoms may come and go; for others, they worsen over time, especially in forms of progressive MS, for which there are no current treatments.

The good news is that decades of research have yielded encouraging results. For example, MS is now diagnosed more quickly, which enables early and ongoing therapy to slow its advancement. There is also growing awareness of its symptoms and ways to address them in order to improve patients' quality of life. At present, there are numerous therapies for treating and managing the disease, with more in development than at any other time in history. And, finally, scientists are making breakthroughs in identifying risk factors that can increase susceptibility to MS, which could lead to more effective prevention.

As the director of the Regional Multiple Sclerosis Center for Neurological Disorders in Milwaukee, Wisconsin, these are the realities I live with every day. I see patients at all stages of MS and other neurological diseases, from the moment they learn of their diagnoses to the end of their lives. Some I treat only briefly; others, I take care of for many years. I see them at their worst and at their best. I share their moments of hope, as well as despair. I know their stories as well as I know my own. And it is those stories that inspired me to write this book.

My patients have been the best teachers I have ever had. They have taught me much of what I know about the art of practicing medicine. They have taught me courage in the face of insurmountable obstacles. They have taught me how powerful the human mind can be, even when the body is failing. And perhaps most importantly, they have helped me understand the many outside influences that affect their care: the role of family members as full-time caregivers; the impact of lawmakers, regulations, and insurance companies on treating patients; and the increasing dependence on technology at the expense of human touch and complete patient histories.

These stories are powerful in themselves, but they take on new meaning in the context of the changing United States' healthcare environment. On one hand, I think you will be as inspired as I am; on the other, you may share my frustration and even anger at some of what I have written. It is my sincere hope that you will learn more about the disease of MS, the many ways in which people live gracefully despite their limitations, the progress of scientific research to find a cure, and the effect of regulations, technology, and external forces on the practice of medicine.

You can read this book from front to back or dip in anywhere you wish, since the stories are not arranged in any particular order.

Caring for patients with neurological disorders, particularly MS, requires more than merely knowing one's specialty. The healthcare environment in which today's physicians find themselves is changing with dizzying speed, not only in terms of medical science, but also in an increasingly complex regulatory, technological, and political context. As physicians attempt to meet more and more demands in less and less time, the practice of traditional medicine is being eroded. Years of hard-won experience are being replaced by computer-generated diagnoses and treatment, which often miss what can only be learned by talking to and touching patients.

Healing the Soul: Unexpected Stories of Courage, Hope, and the Power of Mind addresses these issues head on, while reminding physicians, patients, and caregivers what "the art of medicine" really means.

I. THE POWER OF POSITIVE THINKING

The greatest discovery of all time is that a person can change his future by merely changing his attitude.
—Oprah Winfrey

Beliefs have the power to create and the power to destroy. Human beings have the awesome ability to take any experience of their lives and create a meaning that disempowers them or one that can literally save their lives.
—Anthony Robbins

I t struck her like a tornado, destroying her body as well as her will to live. Until a year ago, she was on the top of the world. Everything was going as she had envisioned her life to be. She loved her job. Having graduated at the head of her class, she was quickly hired as a court reporter in Milwaukee. Her sharp wit and an astonishing performance earned her a favorable footing among colleagues and the legal community. She was also a health fanatic—exercising every day, jogging five miles three times a week, and avoiding non-organic foods as much as possible.

Nothing could go wrong—and yet, it did! A sudden loss of vision in one eye, associated with weakness and numbness on the right side of her body, led to the diagnosis of Multiple Sclerosis (MS). Within only twelve months, she was walking with the assistance of a cane.

MS is the commonest cause of progressive neurological disability in young adults, affecting more than 400,000 people in the United States and 2.3 million worldwide. It strikes patients in the prime of their lives, usually in their second or the third decade, just as they are beginning to start their careers. At age thirty-two, Chris was devastated by a disease that has no cure. She read as much as she could about it.

It was the French neurologist Jean-Martin Charcot who, some 148 years ago, reported in great detail the first case of MS while working at Salpetriere, the world's largest neurological hospital, in Paris. Significant technological advances over the years have made it easier to diagnose MS, but the first FDA-approved therapy came much later, in 1993. In a large, multicenter, a double-blind, randomized, controlled study, this drug was heralded to reduce MS attacks by 30 percent, as well as significantly decrease the disease load abnormalities as measured by magnetic resonance imaging (MRI) of the brain.

In 1999, Chris was diagnosed with severe relapsing-remitting MS and was immediately started on this therapy, which required her to take injections on an ongoing basis. Unfortunately, she didn't respond well to the therapy and continued to have frequent, severe recurrent attacks of her MS. Massive dosages of intravenous corticosteroids, intended to reduce brain inflammation caused by MS lesions, brought about only temporary relief for her disability.

Her life changed completely. She was no longer able to work full time; she could walk a block only with considerable effort; her cognitive function was declining; she could not multitask, a skill that was essential to the career of a successful court reporter.

For Chris, a problem with bladder incontinence was the straw that broke the camel's back. She felt her basic dignity had been snatched away from her. Chemotherapy could bring about some improvement, but it could also lead to some significant short- and long-term complications. After much discussion, Chris felt that doing nothing was not an option. She prepared herself mentally to receive the first dose of anti-cancer therapy for her MS.

It was around this time that we were asked to participate in an international clinical trial to determine the efficacy of natalizumab (now called Tysabri®) in the relapsing form of MS. I immediately thought of Chris and asked her to consider being a study subject, instead of starting chemotherapy. She readily agreed.

* * * * *

The cause of MS is not known. However, advances in the understanding of its pathophysiology have led to some effective therapies. MS is generally believed to be an autoimmune disorder in which the patient's own immune system attacks his or her brain and spinal cord at different sites, causing various symptoms and disabilities. The way the immune system does this is quite tricky. Certain white cells (lymphocytes) in the circulating blood become activated in response to an offending antigen (toxin or foreign substance).

The activated cells promptly migrate into the brain across the blood-brain barrier. Once in the brain, they trigger a cascade of immunological events, which lead to destruction of myelin, the lipid-rich sheath that surrounds nerve fibers and allows smooth and rapid conduction of electrical impulses to occur. Once this crucial insulation is damaged, electrical signals can no longer travel normally between nerve cells. This results in a host of symptoms of MS, like those which affected Chris. Eventually, the nerve fiber itself gets destroyed, leading to permanent disability.

This knowledge led scientists to embark on a long and a remarkable journey to invent a drug that could ultimately block the entry of activated lymphocytes into the brain. The final breakthrough came when three scientists—Drs. Niels K. Jerne, Georges J.F. Köhler, and César Milstein—developed a technique to produce monoclonal antibodies in the laboratory. This technique eventually led to the development of many therapeutic agents for autoimmune disorders and cancer and earned these scientists a Nobel Prize in 1984. A monoclonal antibody is a laboratory-produced molecule that is carefully engineered to attach to a specific protein on immune or cancer cells, causing the cancer cells to become inactive or die. The antibodies act like precision weapons that precisely target abnormal cells in the blood.

Other scientists eventually succeeded in producing a monoclonal antibody (Tysabri®) that would bind to the receptors of activated T cells in blood, thus preventing their entry into the brain. The initial controlled clinical trial of this drug in MS patients showed a dramatic decline in the number of exacerbations, unlike any other drugs used for this disease at the time. Tysabri® was now ready to be tested in a large, double-blind, randomized, controlled study.

A study of this sort follows specific rules to ensure that the results obtained are dependable and free from subject and observer bias. The patient is given either the real medication or a "placebo" (a substance that has no therapeutic effect). Neither the patient nor the clinical evaluator is aware of which drug is dispensed until the study is completed.

"Evidence-based medicine" is considered the gold standard of clinical research. During the last two decades, this term has been linked directly to drugs shown to be effective over a placebo in controlled trials. For obvious reasons, healthcare insurers deny coverage of therapies that are not evidence based, even though such therapies may have been used for years with documented benefit. Controlled clinical trials are a major undertaking and expensive to conduct. It may take ten to fifteen years and more than $800 million to bring a drug to market from the time it is first conceived in the mind of a scientist. Only one in five thousand compounds makes it through discovery, preclinical trials, and review by the U.S. Food and Drug Administration (FDA).

* * * * *

The Tysabri® study protocol was thoroughly discussed with Chris. She would definitely receive the FDA-approved intramuscular injection therapy called Avonex once a week and additionally, either a real drug or a placebo once a month for two years. She was told that she would have a two-to-one chance of receiving real Tysabri® versus the placebo. Chris was ready and began to receive her monthly infusions.

Three months into the clinical trial, Chris was already experiencing positive changes in her MS. There was a noticeable lessening of her fatigue, and her "mental fog" was clearing. She was able to think more clearly and could multitask without any problems. The most dramatic improvement for her was that she was no longer incontinent of urine. By her sixth infusion, Chris was able to walk about a mile a day without having to rest and had begun to work full time. She felt alive again. There were no side effects from the therapy.

Just before her twelfth monthly infusion, she went to the Grand Canyon and hiked into the canyon, carrying a forty-five-pound backpack. She started to jog and ride her bike once again. The designated "blinded" neurologist who evaluated her every three months could no longer detect any abnormalities on her neurological examination!

Even though we were all unaware of the kind of therapy Chris was receiving, we were convinced that she was getting the real drug. For the sake of our other MS patients, who were not doing well with their conventional therapies, we were now hoping that FDA would approve Tysabri® expeditiously. And it did—within a few months. The interim study results were beyond what we had expected them to show. Tysabri® reduced the number of relapses by 67 percent, as well as significantly delayed the progression of disability.

On November 23rd, 2004, the FDA approved the drug based on the extremely positive results from its year-end interim analysis, but insisted that all subjects must complete the remaining second year of study (receiving either a placebo or a real drug) and should be continued to be evaluated in a blinded fashion for the drug's final analysis.

Chris had six months to go. As soon as the pharmaceutical company launched the drug on the market, Tysabri® would become one of the fastest-growing drugs for MS.

And, then, the unthinkable happened. The news shattered our hopes, as well as those of many patients all around the world. Three patients who were receiving Tysabri® had developed a viral infection of the brain called progressive multifocal leukoencephalopathy (PML). This is a fatal condition caused by the JC virus (named after a patient, John Cunningham, in Madison, Wisconsin).

Prognosis for those affected by this illness is grave. Two patients were already dead by the time the news broke. PML, while not uncommon in AIDS patients who are immune-compromised, had never before been seen in MS patients. Tysabri® prevents lymphocytes from gaining entry into the brain and, in a way, does create an immune-compromised state in the central nervous system. But no one saw this coming. The makers of Tysabri® were in shock, but reacted appropriately by immediately recalling the drug from the market worldwide.

The news devastated Chris. She was not very concerned about getting PML; however, the thought that she could no longer get Tysabri® terrified her. She was living proof of what those monthly infusions could do for MS. She now felt scared and powerless. Her plea to the pharmaceutical company to allow her to get the medicine on compassionate grounds, while fully recognizing and accepting the fact that she could develop PML, fell on deaf ears. Maybe indirect pressure from the media might soften the rigid stance taken by the pharmaceutical company, she thought.

The following day, as I sat down for my morning tea and unfolded the newspaper, a large photo of Chris carrying a backpack stared back at me. It was on the front page of the *Kenosha News*. The headline read: "The drug that gave her life back is now snatched away from her." The article went on to discuss in great detail the miraculous recovery Chris had experienced since receiving the drug in the clinical trial.

Headline: The drug that gave her life back is now snatched from her. (Used with permission from the *Kenosha News*)

Later that same morning, I received a list from the pharmaceutical trial coordinator, "unblinding" me as to what my patients had received in the trial. The pharmaceutical company allowed the code to be broken prematurely in light of the PML cases. When I scrolled down the list to Chris, I read, "PLACEBO." I was speechless. That couldn't be true. There must be some error. I had it reconfirmed and, yes, Chris had been receiving placebo injections every month.

Though I didn't know how to break the news to Chris, I did call her right away. There was silence for a moment after I told her. Then she said, "Doc, all I can say is that it was the power of positive thinking that helped me!" Chris went on to tell me that there was not a moment she didn't think that she was receiving the real drug. From day one, she was firmly convinced that she was being treated with the real drug. There had never been a doubt in her mind.

I hung up the phone, but the conversation carried me into a totally different world, a place away from my comfort zone of accepting evidence-based medicine as defined by double-blind, randomized, controlled studies. Is the power of positive thinking so great that it can actually heal the body and brain? How and why did Chris, who had been deteriorating so rapidly both clinically and on MRI scans of her brain, improve so dramatically on placebo therapy? Her brain MRI scans had also shown improvement and stabilization of the disease, despite the fact that she was being treated with a harmless placebo substance. How could this be possible?

* * * * *

My search for answers to these questions eventually led me to believe that healing of the body is a complex process that is greatly influenced by multiple factors, the most important of which is the patient's state of mind. Dr. Albert Schweitzer (1875-1965)—a well-known doctor, humanitarian, and the winner of the 1952 Nobel Peace Prize—said it so beautifully: "Within every patient there resides a doctor, and we as physicians are at our best when we put our patients in touch with the doctor inside themselves."

Norman Cousins (1915-1990), author of the bestselling book, *Anatomy of an Illness*, recognized the importance Dr. Schweitzer's observation and summarized his own thinking as follows: "The greatest force in the human body is the natural drive of the body to heal itself, but that force is not independent of the belief system. Everything begins with a belief."

Chris was so convinced that she was receiving the real treatment that her conscious mind influenced her subconscious mind into believing it as well. Once the subconscious mind takes hold of a suggestion, it sets into motion a chain of events, which eventually, can lead to healing the body and the brain!

The newly recognized field of psychoneuro-immunology (PNI) studies this phenomenon, and some fascinating data are emerging that link a "different state of mind" to invoking a particular immune response. Mental stress or anguish is linked to a not-so-healthy response, while a "happy mind" has the opposite effect.

We are just beginning to understand the scientific basis for what Schweitzer and Cousins knew so many years ago. According to William James, the father of American psychology, the power to move the world is in your subconscious mind. So a placebo is just that, unless it is perceived to be otherwise by the conscious and subconscious mind.

In Chris, the placebo was much more powerful than what we witnessed with the real drug in other patients. Chris somehow was able to change the placebo into something more effective. If this is true, then the notion that subjects can willfully influence how they react to a placebo, questions the validity of the gold standard characterized by a double-blind, placebo-controlled study.

While off placebo therapy, Chris's MS began to deteriorate, requiring frequent IV steroid therapies. Tysabri® was reapproved by the FDA in 2006 and Chris was started on therapy.

* * * * *

One may also argue that this is precisely the reason why well-designed double-blind studies are necessary to ensure that the therapy under study is, indeed, effective. On the other hand, if the ultimate aim is to make a patient better, does it really matter whether that aim is achieved by a proven therapy or by the power of positive thinking? If the power of the subconscious mind is equally therapeutic, then how can a physician influence his or her patients into thinking positively? And even if patients succeed in doing so, can it really make a difference in the eventual outcome of their illnesses?

I was aware of published literature documenting that the survival rate in patients with severe intracerebral bleed was influenced by one variable only. Even though all of the patients in this prospective, multicenter study were treated with a standard protocol, the survival outcome was different at various centers. The only variable linked to a decreased survival rate was whether the treating doctors had "accepted an eventual fatal outcome or not" for their patients. So, if the physician's state of mind can somehow influence the outcome from an illness, how important is it for physicians to invoke and exercise a positive attitude as they attempt to heal their patients? As I struggled with these questions, an occasion arose that led me to an answer.

* * * * *

In April 2005, I was asked to see Bob, a frail, 77-year-old man who was hospitalized because of generalized weakness, double vision, drooping of his eyelids, and shortness of breath. Clinical and laboratory studies quickly confirmed a diagnosis of myasthenia gravis, an autoimmune disorder of unknown cause in which the body produces abnormal antibodies that bind to receptors in muscle. Muscle strength is directly related to physiological binding of a neurotransmitter (acetylcholine) to muscle receptors. However, in myasthenia gravis, the abnormal antibodies block these receptors from responding to normally secreted acetylcholine, thus leading to weakness of varying degrees. Sometimes the weakness can be so severe that it can completely paralyze patients, who then require support from a respirator to keep them alive. Bob was already having some difficulty with breathing and, within a few days, he needed to be placed on a respirator.

Fourteen percent of patients with myasthenia gravis may have a tumor of the thymus gland. This gland resides in the upper front part of the chest. Unfortunately, a large mass was evident on a CT scan of Bob's chest. A needle biopsy proved the mass to be malignant. When the chest was opened, the mass was found to have spread to the surrounding tissues. The surgeon removed as much of the mass as possible without doing damage to vital blood vessels in that region. An oncologist concluded that Bob had stage 4 carcinoma of the thymus gland and recommended a regimen of chemotherapy, with a "guarded prognosis."

Chemotherapy, however, proved to be extremely hard on Bob. He developed all the complications an oncologist dreads seeing. His white blood cells, which fight infection, plummeted to zero. As a result, Bob developed a severe infection requiring strong antibiotics, which in turn, caused further complications. Infection in the gut caused uncontrollable diarrhea and eventually led to massive bleeding.

Bob was the sickest person you would ever see in an intensive care unit. His prognosis was extremely poor. I thought about Chris, who had willfully healed her MS, and I asked myself why Bob couldn't do the same. But how could I get him to think positively when he knew he was dying? This would be a formidable task, especially since he had said final good-byes to his family a number of times. Still, my physician assistant, John Kramer, and I visited Bob twice a day and, with great enthusiasm, telling him that he was indeed getting better each day. We told him that his blood tests were coming back to normal, his chest X-rays showed that his pneumonia was improving, and his respiratory status was recovering faster than we had expected. Even when he went into septic shock and his blood pressure was dangerously low, we kept on telling him that he was recovering and getting better.

Bob had been born and raised in Greece, and at one time, I remember telling him when he was very sick in the ICU that when he returned home, we would have a party and drink ouzo together. Eventually, Bob did get better. He was able to move from the ICU to a regular room and then to his home, exactly three months after he had first been hospitalized for generalized weakness.

Upon his discharge from the hospital, he was asked to return to my outpatient clinic in two weeks for a check-up. I had planned to get a bottle of ouzo for that occasion. He and his wife did show up at the appointed time, but I had forgotten to buy ouzo. Bob looked great. There was no trace of his thymic tumor on the MRI scan of his chest; he was strong and healthy once again. After the examination was over, I got up and gave him a clean bill of health and requested that he make his next appointment in two months.

He grabbed my hand and asked me to sit down. When he removed a bottle of ouzo from a brown bag he was carrying with him, it brought tears to my eyes. I gave him a big hug and, along with my physician assistant, we all had a shot of ouzo behind closed doors.

Robert (Bob) now 87 years old, with the author (March 2014).

Bob is undergoing his monthly plasmapheresis therapy, which removes abnormal antibodies and other toxins from circulation (March 2014).

I had been curious all along whether our positive encouragement to Bob had anything to do with his miraculous recovery, so I asked him for a videotaped interview. He agreed to be interviewed and immediately said that he did not believe us. He had thought that we were out of our minds and that we didn't know what we were saying. But then one day, he said God came to him and whispered in his ears that He was going to give strength to his doctors and that they would make him better. He was told that his doctors were now his "second God" and that he should listen to them and believe in them. After that, he never doubted for a moment that he was going to get better. He could practically see himself walking away from the hospital. Whenever I visited him in the ICU, he would mentally picture himself having a shot of ouzo with me.

That brief "visit from God" transformed his mind-set completely. He started to feel better immediately and, within a week, was able to breathe on his own. He no longer required a respirator. By the second week, he could take food by mouth, and soon, he walked with the aid of a physical therapist.

I did get my question answered! Simply telling a patient to be positive doesn't work. Somehow, the patient needs to be convinced that recovery will occur. Once the conscious mind accepts this as a fact, the subconscious mind then allows healing to take place. However, Bob also stated that, had we not persistently told him he was getting better and he would continue to get better, he was not too sure that God would have come to tell him so!

Bob is now eighty-seven years old and doing extremely well. He remains cancer free. He still continues to drive his car and enjoys growing heirloom tomatoes, the seeds for which he had brought from Greece when he immigrated to this country at the age of twelve. Unfortunately, his wife has now been diagnosed with cancer and Bob—who is now a firm believer in the power of positive thinking and healing—encourages his wife to give it a try.

While this is only one case and would never qualify for evidence-based medicine practice guidelines, I strongly believe that touching a patient with positive energy does wonders for the healing of the body and the soul.

Dr. Vilayanur S. Ramachandran, director of the Center for Brain and Cognition at the University of California, San Diego, has stated it so well: "If you can make a pig speak English by whatever means, you have made your point. You should not have to make a second pig talk to convince the skeptics." However, my statistician friends argue that the "placebo effect" seen in Chris is negated by evenly distributing such subjects in double-blind, randomized, controlled studies and should not cause any problem in defining the efficacy of the treatment under study.

I may be inclined to agree but, as a physician, I am also interested in healing my patients with whatever works and has the least amount of side effects. In Chris, it was her strong belief that turned a placebo into a powerful healing "drug"; in Bob, it was his firm, positive belief in God that healed him.

* * * * *

As we move further into a more remote telemedicine and computer-driven interactions with our patients and evidence-based medicine to guide our choice of therapies for our patients, I am afraid we will forget to listen to the reasons we became physicians in the first place. I submit that positive thoughts and energy are a powerful therapy that can promote healing and that there lies a vast, uncharted field that needs continued exploration by the medical establishment.

There is no doubt that newer therapies and medical technologies have revolutionized the way we practice medicine; they do offer better outcomes. However, the importance of *how* these therapies are delivered to patients is also significant. How that therapy is perceived by the patient has the potential to produce either a negative or a positive outcome. A strong and unwavering belief that healing will occur is crucial.

A physician hands over a lot more than just a prescription. A physician's attitude also becomes a part of that therapy. Despite our telling Bob, whom we assumed was vulnerable to our daily suggestions, that he was healing, that message had no effect on him. He said so when I interviewed him. It was only when God came to him that he finally was convinced that, indeed, he would heal. The reason I suspect he didn't believe us was because we didn't really believe what we were telling him. We had perceived a grim prognosis for Bob; somehow, he could sense that negative energy even as we tried to coat it with positive words.

There is a lot of wisdom in what William Osler (1849-1919), the father and one of the greatest icons of modern medicine had to say: "A young physician starts life with twenty treatments for each disease, while the old physician ends life with one treatment for twenty diseases." This is even more relevant now than ever before. The impact of holding a patient's hand and approaching that patient with positive thoughts is so powerful; yet, that is not taught in medical schools. There is a great emphasis on drugs for a quick fix, and with an increasing reliance on computerized electronic systems guiding young physicians in the practice of medicine, they may find that even twenty treatments are not enough to treat a disease.

For many patients, oomph and positive support are the most powerful medicines. I do not mean to debunk modern medicine and the wonderful break-throughs that have been made over the years. I am merely suggesting that we, as physicians, should remember how important attitude—ours and our patients'—is in the healing process. Sometimes, it needs a boost from science, but sometimes, it is all that is required.

2. UNFINISHED BUSINESS

I touch you knowing we weren't born tomorrow,
and somehow, each of us will help the other live,
and somewhere, each of us must help the other die.
—Adrienne Rich, *Twenty-One Love Poems*

Death is not the greatest loss in life.
The greatest loss is what dies inside us while we live.
—Norman Cousins, *Anatomy of an Illness*

The recommendation of the hospital's Utilization Review Committee kept coming back to me as I walked toward the intensive care unit (ICU): "She is ready to be transferred to a nursing home that will accept patients on a respirator."

As a treating neurologist, I could see the committee's concerns. Arita had accumulated a huge bill, and since she was on welfare, the hospital was likely to be reimbursed only marginally.

I entered her room, and her eyes followed me as I walked around the bed to check the respirator settings. Once again, she had made no progress. She remained totally respirator-dependent.

I knew she would still be looking at me when I finally turned to face her. I tried to read her eyes.

Arita was only thirty-four; yet, MS had totally paralyzed her. I knew that she was making every attempt
to bring her thoughts to her eyes for me to read.

What I saw in her eyes wasn't sadness. It was not
anger. It certainly was not "I have given up, Doc." I
had seen that same look in her eyes many times since
she had been put on a respirator eighty-four days
previously. Invariably, I would see those eyes as I
drove home each evening.

I had taken care of Arita from the time she first
came into my office with a walker in 1984. "I will go
back to fixing cars one day," she had declared. "I will
not give up!"

Despite her progressive deterioration, Arita's visits
to the clinic were always uplifting for me and for my
staff. A few months before the exacerbation that put
her on a respirator, she had wheeled herself in and
asked jokingly, "Doc, I may be fat, but don't you think
I am too young to be a grandma?" I looked at the
photo she showed me of her granddaughter, closely
held against her face. Arita looked very happy.

It was winter 1990, and as she lay there looking at
me, I took her hand in my hands and mentally
rehearsed how best to tell her. "Arita," I began.
"Because of the permanent damage to your brain, you
will most likely remain on a respirator for the rest of
your life. You may not be able to talk, eat, or move

your arms and legs again, but your mind will remain intact. Do you understand me?" I asked.

She nodded her head slightly to say yes. "While you are here with us, Arita, should your heart stop for any reason, do you want us to do all we can to get it going again or let nature take its course?"

As she continued to look into my eyes, tears welled up in hers, rolled down her cheeks, and onto her pillow. She turned to the nurse, who knew what she wanted: an alphabet board so she could spell out her reply to my question.

"If my heart stops, I want a heart and lung transplant," was her answer.

Obviously, Arita was not ready to be moved to a nursing home. The fight was not over. As I walked out, I felt as if my job were unfinished. I knew I had done all that could be done for her physical being, but her inner self, her soul, I had failed to heal. And those eyes ... they made me uneasy. I knew they were telling me something.

On my way home one evening not long after that event, I impulsively got off the expressway and headed back to the hospital. I walked to Arita's room, gently put my hand on her head, and asked, "Are you scared? Are you afraid to die?"

After she picked up the last S from the board to say "Y-E-S," she turned to me.

I didn't know what to say. My medical training had not prepared me for this. I found myself tightening my grip on her hand, but at the same time, I knew I was offering only a false sense of security. I remembered my mentor's words: "If you can't do anything to save your patients, then at least hold their hands and be there."

I had not known Arita to be religious, or at least we never talked about her belief system. I didn't know how she would react, but still I asked, "Is it okay if I get a priest to talk to you for a little while?"

Father Joe, I knew, was still in the hospital. When he heard about Arita, he said, "Doctor, go home. I will talk to her."

At 7:00 that evening, Father Joe called me at home to say that he had a long chat with Arita and that she was at ease. A few hours later, I was awakened from a deep sleep by the ring of a telephone. It was Kathy, an ICU nurse. "Arita passed away in her sleep," Kathy said.

I couldn't sleep much that night. Many thoughts swirled around in my head. It is impressive to order today's sophisticated lab tests and to use complex medical computers in routine clinical practice. But as daylight broke, I realized that, as my mentor had said, "To be a physician, you have to hold your patients' hands and learn to read their eyes." As a physician, it felt good to know that I had not failed to treat Arita, the person, but I was also troubled by the fact that it took me so long to read the message in her eyes. Her soul had needed to be healed before she could let go. Medical school and residency training prepare us to treat the ailing body with many different therapies, but nothing teaches us how to read the eyes!

* * * * *

A few years later and eight thousand miles away, I witnessed something that caused me to pause and appreciate the power of mind over body. It also brought back memories of Arita.

A day and a half after I received the call about my father's deteriorating medical condition, I was in India at his bedside. The end was near, and we both knew it. At age ninety-three, even though his mind was alive, his body was failing. On the third day of his stay in the ICU, my father looked at me and said, "Take me home."

His eyes remained focused on mine. He wasn't ordering me to do it, and he wasn't pleading. The tone of his voice was one I had heard before in my patients who knew that they were dying and had to convey an important message—their last wish. I recognized that tone in his voice.

Almost immediately, this put me in a different state of mind. My father was putting all his trust in me; now it was up to me to do the right thing. Those three words awakened feelings in me that I had never before experienced. Was this the last of the many bonds that complete a father-son relationship? I instantly felt privileged and also very sad because it became very clear to both of us that his long journey on this earth would be over in just a few days. I felt as if I had become my father's father. I couldn't fail him in his last days.

"Yes, we will go home," I said, as I squeezed his hand lightly to let him know that he could count on me.

Four of us carried him from the ambulance into the house and placed him on his bed. He smiled as his head rested on his favorite pillow. He always carried that pillow with him when he traveled, even when he visited us in the United States from India. I hooked him up to an intravenous drip to keep him hydrated. He had not been able to swallow for a few days. Most of my brothers and sisters had flown to India from overseas to be with him, and he was happy to see them.

By that afternoon, he had become quite lethargic but opened his eyes occasionally to look around and ask for my sister Illa, who was still in America, hastily arranging for a flight to India. It was Sunday, and she had to wait until Monday to get an Indian visa before an airline would issue her a ticket.

The following day, my father looked even worse. His kidneys had failed, and his serum potassium level was rising to a critical level. He was not making any urine. He was no longer responding to his name. In the evening, he opened his eyes and once again asked for Illa. She was expected to land in Mumbai the following morning and then would have to catch a domestic flight to arrive home around noon. I am not sure if he could hear us, but we kept telling him that Illa would be home soon. That night and the following morning, we couldn't get much response from him.

One of our friends was waiting at the airport to bring Illa as soon as she landed. At half past twelve, we heard the beeping of the car horn, signaling that Illa was here. We rushed her to the bedside, where she put her head on our father's chest and said, "Bapuji, I am here!"

We were all gathered around the bed, hoping that he would open his eyes and see her. And he did. He smiled at her but was unable to talk. Illa had brought the Cadbury's hazelnut chocolate he liked. She broke off a tiny piece and offered it to him. He opened his mouth and took it. Half an hour later, he lapsed into a coma and passed away that afternoon.

Both my father and Arita were able to prolong the moment of their deaths willfully. Arita was afraid to die, to let go, while my father waited for his daughter to arrive. I had witnessed similar situations in a few of my patients, but had never paid much attention to what was happening.

* * * * *

I seriously began to question whether a dying person could choose his or her final moment. If this is possible, then, is there a way to postpone death for an extended period of time? Can patients be trained or motivated to do so? If so, while this might not help 10 percent of people who die suddenly, for the remaining 90 percent, it could change everything. They could be given a chance to address some of the most important issues on their minds before they died. Can the timing of death be personalized to take care of "unfinished business"?

Healthcare providers who work at hospice facilities provided some of the answers to my questions. "We see it very often," was the unanimous answer I received from more than thirty such professionals I interviewed. These hospice healthcare workers, who provide comfort and tend to the emotional and spiritual needs of those who are dying, had jointly witnessed 780 deaths. All of them agreed that, yes, those who are dying can purposefully prolong their lives from a few days to up to a month. The most common driving forces seemed to be waiting for their loved ones to arrive, seeking closure of some sort, or an important anniversary date. If they verbally declare their wish, the majority of them are able to prolong their lives and die immediately after the anticipated event has occurred.

"Sometimes, they become very lucid when the person they are waiting for arrives and soon after greeting that person, lapse into a coma and die. The family members find this difficult to accept, for they interpret the improvement as an indication that the patient is getting better," some of the hospice nurses told me. "Quite often, a loved one may hold vigil for days, step out of the room for just a moment, and that is when the dying person passes away. It is supposedly to protect the loved ones from letting them see when the person takes his or her last breath."

All of the care workers I spoke with felt very strongly that the family members can influence the dying person to prolong life. If they urge their loved ones to live a little longer for a special event or to wait for a family member who is in transit, that person may be able to stay alive.

"Sometimes, family members simply do not give their loved ones permission to die. These patients tend to linger on until some sort of closure has occurred," according to a nurse who had witnessed more than 200 deaths.

As physicians, we must be prepared to assist our patients and their families in making and acting on these crucial decisions. Holding off drugs that may cause a drop in blood pressure or lead to drowsiness should be avoided if the dying patient is waiting for a loved one to arrive. Sometimes, supporting the dying patient with a stimulant drug may be necessary to assist the patient in achieving fulfillment of his or her last wish.

According to one of the hospice nurses, if the patient has declared his or her final wish, psychological help to gently keep the patient's focus on what is important in the last few hours of the person's death can be of tremendous help and rewarding, for the one who is dying and for the loved ones as well. This was true in my father's case. We kept telling him where my sister was every few hours on her journey and when she would arrive home. I am sure this helped him to hang on just a little longer because he passed away just a few hours after he had greeted her.

Finally, for those patients who are comatose, I wonder if there is a way to influence their survival or postpone death. Family members frequently find their decreasing ability to communicate very distressing. The last hours of life are the time when they most want to communicate with their loved one. Can death indeed be prolonged by family members or healthcare providers?

These are important but difficult questions to answer. We do not know if unconscious patients can actually hear and it is difficult to clinically assess comprehension of such a dying patient. There have not been any scientific studies that would authoritatively answer these questions. According to the hospice workers with a combined total of over 230 years of practice, the feeling was unanimous. All of them indicated that unconscious patients can perceive and sense the energy around them. They are able to prolong life!

A well-known neurologist and a respected medical ethicist, Dr. Michael P. McQuillen, shared this story with me:

> On one occasion (while making clinical rounds at the University of Kentucky Medical Center), we stopped at the bedside of a young man who was in coma after a traumatic brain injury. He had not improved over several days and, while his examination did not fit the criteria for "brain dead," it was unlikely that he would improve. ICU beds were in short supply at the time, so the suggestion was made that he be taken off the ventilator to "let nature take its course" and free up a sorely-needed ICU bed.
>
> A medical student with the rounding team exclaimed, "You can't do that. His mother is coming up from their home in eastern Kentucky; she has to embrace a warm body!"

It was a full day or more before the
patient's mother arrived. It was not until she
whispered "goodbye" in her son's ear and gave
him a big hug that his heart stopped. They did
not have to take him off the ventilator.

The research related to unconscious awareness is
ongoing. It is now well accepted that hearing is the
last sense to go when a person becomes unconscious.
How and what you say in the presence of such a
patient is very important. A number of studies have
reported that, after regaining consciousness, some
patients said they heard and understood various
conversations that took place while they were unconscious. Unlike the conscious, the subconscious mind
never sleeps. It holds all awareness that is not presently in the conscious mind. All memories, emotions,
feelings, and thoughts are stored in the subconscious
mind. It has memory of every event we have ever
experienced.

Is this the reason that a person—conscious or
unconscious—who is holding a single thought before
he dies can actually tap into his subconscious mind
and his last wish? The conscious mind has been
compared, metaphorically, to the tip of an iceberg,
whereas the subconscious is likened to the huge
mass below the surface.

William James (1842–1910), the father of American psychology, had this to say: "The power to move the world is in your subconscious mind."

At the 22nd Annual Meeting of the Associated Professional Sleep Societies, 2008, in Baltimore, Maryland, Allan Hobson, a world authority on consciousness, said, "Even when consciousness is largely obliterated, the brain remains highly active and is still capable of processing its own information."

When a person is unconscious, there are parts of the brain that continue to monitor and assess the outside and inside worlds. Using functional MRI of the brain, which measures blood flow as a surrogate for brain activity, scientists were able to show significant brain activity in the late former Israeli Prime Minister, Ariel Sharon, when his son spoke to him, but not when random speech was presented to him. This was a significant finding, since the Prime Minister had been in a vegetative-state coma for eight years and had been kept alive by a respirator. The two-hour test was led by a team of Israeli and American scientists.

"Information from the external world was transferred to the appropriate parts of Mr. Sharon's brain," said team member Martin Monti, assistant professor of cognitive psychology at the University of California, Los Angeles. "However, the evidence did not indicate as clearly whether Mr. Sharon consciously perceived this information."

Besides hearing, touch in an unconscious patient should be regarded as an important form of communication. In another experiment conducted on Mr. Sharon, a positive response to tactile stimulation was also detected. The majority of the nurses I interviewed indicated that they have seen a calming effect on patients when loved ones touch or hold their hands. A few, however, have witnessed just the opposite effect—patients can become more agitated, their heart rate goes up, and they start to breathe faster. The touch, the nurses all agreed, is a powerful way to communicate with an unconscious person.

A few of the nurses observed that comatose patients are able to perceive the presence of their loved ones in the room even when they are not talking to or touching the patients. As soon as family members leave the room, the patients' vital signs change dramatically but then tend to normalize when they return. How is this possible? Is there energy or vibration patients can perceive from their loved ones? Are their subconscious minds, which have been primed with this information for years, still "awake" and therefore able to recognize the presence of that energy?

I have always been amazed how my elderly patients who have been living together for more than four to five decades can communicate with each other without much verbal, visual, or tactile communication. When I have a very hard time hearing the soft, low-volume speech, I usually turn to the patient's spouse, who can tell me exactly what the patient is saying! I doubt very much that the spouse, who also happens to be hearing impaired, actually heard the "speech." How is it, then, that they can hear but I cannot? Is it the energy they perceive and register rather than the actual "sound of the speech"? If so, is it then possible that when patients are unconscious, their subconscious minds can still perceive that energy from their loved ones?

I give frequent educational talks to patients with MS and their family members. To explain the presence and importance of the kind of "energy" in an environment, I usually ask, "Those of you who have been living together for some time, please raise your hands if you can tell that your spouse or partner is in angry mood when you have just entered the house, but have not yet spoken to or seen your partner?" There is laughter in the group as all of the hands shoot up! I believe that thoughts can emit energy, which can be felt as negative or positive by an unconscious person.

There is no scientific evidence for this as yet, but based on their personal experiences, Deepak Chopra and Wayne Dyer have shown that there is an increase in "a happy neurotransmitter" called serotonin, not only in a group of people who are meditating but also in others residing in the vicinity and are unaware that the meditation going on. Positive, happy, and calming thoughts can influence people in your immediate vicinity. If this is true, then it is important not only for the family and friends, but also for the treating physicians to have positive thoughts when around those who are in need of that extra boost!

Science certainly lends support to what the hospice healthcare workers have witnessed. Family members can influence comatose patients by touching and talking to them. They can even influence dying patients to prolong their lives or, in some instances, to let go, as was the case with the traumatic brain-injury patient in Kentucky. Even though he was almost brain dead, he "heard" the medical student say that his mother was on her way to say goodbye. He waited until his mother gave him the permission to die.

The above discussion leads me to believe that people who are dying can prolong their own lives for a short time, at least until a strong desire is fulfilled. They can be influenced by their loved ones, even if they are comatose. But most important, even if they are unconscious, their subconscious minds are active and able to perceive and process information. That's why a supportive and a positive attitude toward the dying is so important.

As they are able to delay the moment of their deaths, I wonder if some people also have a fleeting awareness of what they have left undone in their lives. The last thing my father did was taste a small piece of the chocolate my sister, Illa, had given him. He left the rest, as we all will leave the unfinished business of our lives when we die. Few of us depart with everything we ever meant to do wrapped up in a neat package. There is always something we didn't get to do or perhaps didn't even think about. Let us hope that we can leave the "unfinished chocolate" behind without regrets and exit the world remembering the sweet taste of life.

3. THE WILL TO LIVE!

*I've learned from experience that the greater part of
our happiness or misery depends on our dispositions
and not on our circumstances.*
—Martha Washington (1731-1802); U.S. First Lady

often think about Laura. I first met her thirty years ago when she was twenty-four and full of life. An avid fan of Harley Davidson, she was the only woman I knew who owned a Harley motorcycle. She was very proud of her bike, which she had bought with money saved while waiting tables at an upscale restaurant in Milwaukee, Wisconsin. She did not own a car. The bike was her means of transportation; and on the weekends, she would ride long distances, sometimes up to two hundred miles a day.

Laura loved every minute of it. The bike was her passion. She could tell me everything there was to know of Harley Davidson—how the business was started in a small shed in 1903 by William S. Harley and two brothers, Arthur and Walter Davidson, in a place not too far from where she lived in Milwaukee.

By 1920, Harley Davidson was the largest manufacturer of motorcycles in the entire world with dealerships in sixty-seven countries. They also had experienced a 5,000 percent increase in total sales. Harley-Davidson went on to become the gold standard for all other motorcycles. In World War I, over 20,000 of the Harley bikes were used for military purposes. The Harley Davidson was known to be among the fastest bikes and was the first to ever win a race with a speed topping 100 mph.

Laura would amuse me with the history and mechanical details of all the models produced up to that point and name the most popular Harley riders, both men and women. Not only did Laura enjoy riding the bike, she also thoroughly knew her "Harley," as she lovingly called it. It was while she was on her bike that she first developed the initial symptoms of a disease that would eventually rob her of all her bodily functions.

It was a hot summer day in Wisconsin. Laura had been riding for about two hours. She was thirsty and decided to pull over at the next gas station to get a bottle of water. She parked her bike, took off her helmet, and as she came off her bike, she collapsed on the ground. Her legs would not support her body. She felt a strange, electrical buzzing feeling from her waist down. Initially, she didn't think much about it. She had experienced similar symptoms in the past, especially after driving her bike long distances, but never this intensely.

"My legs must have gone to sleep from riding this long," she thought.

After waiting on the ground for some time and massaging her legs, she tried to get up. Once again, her legs were like "wet noodles." She couldn't manage it. She panicked.

Many thoughts raced through Laura's mind. Had she had a stroke? Would she be able to walk and ride her bike again? The fear she experienced was unlike any she had ever known. She felt as if her body was sinking into the earth and suffocating her. As she gathered all her strength and tried to get up again, her legs didn't move at all. She reached out to feel her legs and found that her slacks were wet; she had lost control over her bladder. She let out a huge cry, and moments later, she passed out.

I first met Laura in an emergency room of the County Hospital in Milwaukee. I had just completed my first-year training in neurology and was on call the evening paramedics wheeled Laura into the ER. The manager of the gas station had called an ambulance when he found her unconscious in his parking lot. The ER doctor had paged me a few minutes earlier to inform me that a young woman with an acute onset of paralysis in both her legs was being brought to the ER; he wanted a neurological consultation.

Quickly, I obtained a pertinent history from her. She had had episodes of numbness and tingling in her lower extremities in the past, but nothing like this. She had been in perfect health and had never been hospitalized, except when she gave birth to her son three years ago. Now, she complained of intense tingling in her legs. She was paralyzed from the waist down and she had no control over her bladder.

After I had completed my clinical examination, I sat down to prepare a list of possible diagnoses. She was a young Caucasian female, born and raised in Wisconsin, who had developed significant weakness in her legs with bladder incontinence after she had been driving in hot and humid weather. In the hour she had been in the air-conditioned environment, the strength in her legs had improved slightly, and the numbness began to subside. Immediately, I began to think of a possible diagnosis that I secretly hoped was incorrect.

Laura was hospitalized. After a thorough neurological examination, and based on the findings on the CT scan of her brain (MRI, though invented, had yet to be used in healthcare), some blood work, and spinal-fluid results, my clinical suspicion was confirmed. How could I tell her the diagnosis? She was so young and vibrant and full of energy. Every time I visited her, she would talk to me about her bike and how she hoped that she would be healed way before the winter snow arrived so that she could still ride her bike that year.

She responded well to intravenous steroids. She could now walk with a walker. Her bladder function had improved, but she still suffered from urinary urgency and occasional incontinence.

"Laura," I said, setting down in a chair I had pulled toward her bed to be near her. "We have reviewed all your test results, and we know what is causing the weakness in your legs." In order to tell patients truthfully and frankly about their diagnosis, it is vital to acquire the necessary skills to communicate the bad news in a sensitive manner and to support patients once the diagnosis is clear. It is a skill that is learned through experience, but it never gets any easier when it is time to share the diagnosis with the patient. I had rehearsed and revised many times in my mind, what and how to say it to Laura.

"So then, you can fix me ... right?" she asked. I replied, "Laura, you have Multiple Sclerosis. This is a disease that will stay with you for the rest of your life. There is no cure. MS is considered to be an immune-mediated disease in which the body's immune system mistakenly attacks myelin—the covering of the nerve fibers—and eventually the nerve fibers themselves in the brain, the spinal cord, and the optic nerves.

Laura was speechless. I continued. "It can get worse to the point at which you could become wheelchair bound. Since the brain, spinal cord, and the optic nerves control all of your bodily functions, you may have multiple and different symptoms, depending on where the abnormal antibodies attack. It is difficult to say if and when the attacks may happen, but in the meantime, a good healthy lifestyle will definitely help. Exercise daily, and eat fresh, nutritious foods. If you have another attack, we could treat you with a powerful group of anti-inflammatory drugs called steroids to hasten the recovery process, but there is no treatment available to prevent you from having further MS attacks or slow the progression of the disease."

Laura was already working with a rehabilitation specialist and was being taught the exercises she could do on her own once she went home. In the United States, MS is the commonest cause of progressive neurological disability in young adults.

Despite the years of intense research, the first approved therapy, which could reduce the number of MS relapses by 30 percent, would come to market fourteen years later. At that time, the only therapy we could offer Laura was supportive care. If she had another MS attack, steroids and sometimes anti-cancer drug therapy to kill the cells that produce offending antibodies, could be considered.

Laura stared down at her legs and was silent for a long time. Finally, she looked up at me. She had been crying silently. I took her hand in mine and reassured her that a lot of research was being done to find an effective therapy and even a cure for MS.

"There is hope!" I insisted. She should live each day to its fullest and consider each day as a gift from God. After that, I couldn't say much to her. But I was surprised at myself for what I had said and how I had said it. Never before had I conveyed sad news to a patient all by myself. It was a strange experience. I was able to connect with Laura without saying too much. I could sense that she felt my pain and concern for her while I was talking to her.

It is the moment that every physician in training hopes to experience at some time during his or her schooling: how to communicate sad news in a manner that fosters comfort, trust, and a genuine sense of security in a patient.

Laura and I sat in silence for a while. She slowly reached out for my hand, held it tightly in hers, and finally spoke. "Can you be my doctor?" she asked. "Will you take care of me?" Little did I realize how the simple nodding of my head that day would teach me so much over the years to come. Laura was my first MS patient. She drew me into that disease; now I care for more than four thousand MS patients and direct one of the largest MS centers in the country.

In the subsequent fifteen years, Laura taught me what I had never learned in medical school. Any doctor can write a prescription for a wheelchair, but

Laura made me understand what it really means to give up walking. The resultant emotional stress is something only a patient can experience and express, and she did this graciously and with a positive attitude, rather than feeling sorry for herself.

"My time to walk on this earth has come to an end. I will now explore it with an electric wheelchair," she said. "It will be so much more fun to go out shopping to the malls now that I don't have to worry about pushing a walker!"

But behind her positive statement, I knew very well how much she had suffered at giving up walking, even though it was with a walker. Every time she was forced to relinquish a bodily function, she would recognize that MS was taking a toll on her, but she would move on and focus on things she could still do. She truly made me understand the statement I had initially thrown at her— "Live each day to its fullest!"

Whenever I feel "down" or start to complain about some bothersome but trivial issues, I think about Laura. Knowing how she overcame and adapted to her progressive disability always inspires me to take this in stride and to focus on positive things. It always works for me.

Gradually, Laura's bladder ceased to respond to medications, and she required a major surgery to create an external pouch, using parts of her intestines to collect urine from her kidneys. The pouch is emptied mechanically several times a day. One day, she was admitted on an emergency basis because of a bowel obstruction due to "sluggish guts." She required an immediate colostomy, which stayed with her for the rest of her life. By then, Laura was confined to bed and was beginning to have swallowing problems. As a result, she contracted frequent aspiration pneumonia. She could no longer take anything orally, necessitating a feeding tube for all of her nourishment.

The most challenging problem, however, had yet to come. Laura began to have muscle spasms in her legs, which progressively got worse despite massive amounts of different muscle relaxers. She would cry out in pain when they intensified. She described the pain as that associated with a bad muscle cramp, except that she experienced that degree of pain for twenty hours a day! The drugs made her groggy; she didn't like that, either. MS did not rob her of her mind, and she was very proud of that. She would endure the pain but could not stand the drugs that were "stealing" her mind. The spasms in her legs caused her legs to bend forcibly toward her chest, thereby tearing the skin over her knees and hip joints. Eventually, she got some relief after the surgeons cut some of the tendons and bones in her legs.

I remember very well the Christmas Eve of 1991. Laura's mother telephoned me to say that her daughter was having some difficulty with breathing. My heart sank! Was this the end for Laura? Mortality in MS is usually due to lung infection, which leads to poor respiration in a patient who is already physically debilitated by the illness.

An ambulance was dispatched to bring her to the hospital immediately. I was waiting for her when she arrived at the ER. Laura looked at me, smiled a little, and barely whispered to me, "I can't die without wishing you a Merry Christmas!" Her blood gases looked bad and without being connected to an artificial respirator, she would not make it. I explained all this to her and also warned her that, once she was connected to a respirator, she might not be able to live without it. Laura had made up her mind. She wanted to live! She left the hospital two weeks later with a respirator connected to her and remained respirator dependent for the rest of her life.

Whenever she came to the clinic for her follow-up visits, Laura was always well dressed, well groomed, and looked pretty with the right amount of make-up. She wore different jewelry every time I saw her. And she did all this even though she was completely paralyzed from the neck down! She had trained her caregivers well.

I always marveled at how, despite her disability, she managed to live her life so joyfully. Her face would break out in a big smile when I truthfully told her that she was my best-looking and best-dressed patient. I always made it a point to see her promptly whenever she came to the clinic, recognizing that it was difficult for her to sit in a chair for any length of time.

One day, she had to wait for an extended period of time, and when I finally went in to see her, I had goose bumps when I saw what she was doing. She was going through a home-improvement magazine and directing her aide to cut out pictures of homes she liked and paste them in an album. I didn't know what to say. My eyes moistened a little at the realization that, despite her severe disability, Laura was still teaching me how to live!

"You have to dream and live your dreams, even if it is in your imagination," she said. Despite being paralyzed from below the neck and dependent on the respirator, unable to swallow and requiring a permanent feeding tube, with a colostomy and a pouch to collect her feces and urine, she had continued to subscribe to a home-improvement magazine!

The year 1993 was both bad and good for Laura. She was in the hospital because of an infected pressure sore in her back. A scan revealed that her bones below the wound were infected. Unfortunately, the strong antibiotics required to fight the infection caused serious complications, and she became gravely ill. She pulled through this bout, but we all knew that her time on this earth was fast coming to an end.

She was discharged to a sub-acute facility, where she would receive ongoing intravenous therapy for her bone infection. She did well for a while but had to be readmitted to the ICU for pneumonia in May 1993. While she was critically ill, Milwaukee was getting ready for the biggest Harley-Davidson function in its history.

I was examining Laura when she heard the news on TV of the upcoming Harley-Davidson event, which would celebrate the company's ninetieth anniversary in Milwaukee with a "Harley family" reunion. Harley enthusiasts from around the word would be travelling to Milwaukee. An estimated one hundred thousand people were expected to ride in a parade of motorcycles.

I looked at Laura, and our eyes locked. I saw a sparkle in her eyes I hadn't seen for a very long time. It had been her dream to ride in one of Harley's big parades and festivals. But how could she do it? She was on a respirator, quadriplegic, and very ill. She had been in the intensive care unit for the past three weeks.

"Be sure to watch it on television. You do not want miss this big one!" I said as I left her room. I could see tears forming in her eyes, and now for the first time, I didn't have the courage to stay with her. I knew how much she loved her bike, and over the years, she had told me more than I had cared to know about Harley Davidson. The biggest Harley parade was to take place in her hometown, and she was stuck in the ICU.

I had been with her at all her major surgeries, taken care of her many times when she became gravely ill, and held her hand when we thought she was going to die. But now, I just couldn't face her. I didn't have the courage to be with her. It was painful for me to see her in the ICU bed when the record-breaking, history-making Harley function was about to take place practically in her backyard.

That sparkle in her eyes had been her soul speaking to me. Even though MS ravaged her body, her soul had not been touched by this devil. What a powerful lesson to learn! And yet, emotionally, I was not prepared to embrace the most valuable lesson Laura was teaching me in the final few days of her life. I knew I had done whatever I could to heal her body, but I was totally unprepared for this. I cried that evening, thinking about her and how helpless I felt that her last wish—to be in the Harley parade—would not be realized.

And then it hit me like a brick! Even though physically she might be dying, her spirit was alive! She had endured all of the major physical catastrophes hurled at her by MS, and now, in her final days, she certainly did not have to give up her spirit simply because she was physically disabled. She always maintained that, she had MS, but MS did not have her!

With the help of the hospital administrators, an ambulance company that provided a van equipped with a respirator, and grateful accommodations by the Harley Davidson Parade organizers, Laura rode in the parade that weekend! The ambulance doors and windows were kept open, so she could watch the more than one hundred thousand bikers riding with her! The thunder of those bikes caused her whole body to come alive. She enjoyed every minute of the ride. Not only did she dream the dream, she lived it!

Laura passed away at the age of forty-two in 1998. A very appropriate epitaph on her tombstone would be:

And fear not them which kill the body, but are not able to kill the soul: but rather fear him which is able to destroy both soul and body in hell.
—Matthew 10:28 (KJV)

Laura on her wedding day
with her mother, Lilian.

Laura and her new husband on their wedding day.

Laura in 1979, the year she was diagnosed with multiple sclerosis.

Laura and the author in her hospital room the year she was diagnosed with MS (1979).

Laura in her wheelchair.
Lilian sitting on her beloved Harley (1983).

Laura is quadriplegic and needs a respirator to breathe (early 1990s).

Lilian has saved the leather jackets Laura used to wear while riding her Harley.

The author visiting with Lilian, now 86 years old (January, 2014).

Laura Hoye
1956–1998

4. THE LOST ART OF TOUCH

If we can make the correct diagnosis, the healing can begin.
If we can't, both our personal health
and our economy are doomed.
—Andrew Weil, MD

Our sorrows and wounds are healed
only when we touch them with compassion.
—Buddha

There is no more difficult art to acquire than the
art of observation. The value of experience is not in
seeing much, but in seeing wisely."
—Sir William Osler

Sandra was new to our clinic. The nurse had summarized her medical history in one small paragraph for me to review before I saw her. At age forty-six, she had been confined to a wheelchair for six years, had been blind in both eyes for a year and a half, and had undergone surgery to have a catheter inserted into her bladder to drain and collect her urine in an external plastic bag. Sandra was diagnosed to be suffering from a progressive form of MS. She was referred to me because of severe muscle spasms in her legs.

Conventional therapy had failed. Her internist had suggested an intrathecal baclofen pump to control the disabling muscle spasticity in her legs. This implantable medical device requires a surgical procedure, which delivers very small quantities of medication directly into a patient's spinal fluid via a small catheter connected to a metal pump that stores the medication. This device is a godsend to such patients. The therapeutic effect is dramatic; it significantly improves the quality of life. The pump has a computer that "talks" to an external hand-held device so that the rate of medication delivered can be easily regulated to achieve optimal control of muscle spasticity. The surgery to implant the device, and the device itself, sound very complex; however, the side effects are actually minimal.

Sandra's immediate problem should be easy to fix, I said to myself as I gathered my instruments and started to walk towards her room. I was more concerned about her MS, which had steadily robbed her of her bodily functions and caused her to become severely disabled since she was diagnosed seven years ago.

Sandra was sitting in a motorized wheelchair; a see-through plastic tube was draining her urine into a bag attached to the side of the wheelchair. She was wearing dark sunglasses. I introduced myself and extended my hand toward her.

"Very pleased to meet you, but I cannot see your hand," she said, starting to feel the space in front of her with her right hand.

I shook her hand and then sat down to take a detailed medical history, which is really the most important part of a neurological examination. As a neurologist, I had been taught not to proceed with the physical examination of a patient until I had arrived at a short list of possible diagnoses based on the patient's symptoms. Initially, it seemed very straightforward. I had been told that Sandra had MS, but as I listened to her and asked more questions, I began to doubt that diagnosis.

Over the past twenty-five years, I have seen and examined thousands of patients with MS, but Sandra was different. I just did not feel comfortable with her given diagnosis. As I observed her body language and the way she answered some pointed questions, I was more convinced that the new diagnosis forming in my mind was the correct one.

One hundred years ago, Sir William Osler, a Canadian physician and one of the four founding professors of Johns Hopkins Hospital, said:

> Medicine is learned by the bedside and not in the classroom. Let not your conceptions of disease come from words heard in the lecture room or read from the book. See, and then reason and compare and control. But see first.

These words are still worth heeding.

True to the history offered by the nurse, Sandra was blind. She could not even perceive light shone directly into her eyes. She could not lift her legs off the floor. She could not walk. Loss of bladder function was evident by the catheter surgically implanted above her pelvic bone. Yet, after I had finished examining her, I was convinced that she did not have MS. In fact, I did not think that she had any organic disease of her brain or spinal cord. I also knew that she was not "faking it." So, how could I explain the progressive decline in her bodily functions over the last seven years?

We all know that the brain and spinal cord (in essence, the central nervous system) control all of our bodily functions. Pathological changes at multiple sites in the central nervous system, such as those seen in MS, could certainly explain Sandra's disability. Yet, the MRI scans of her brain and spinal cord, which by now should have shown MS lesions, were completely normal! Could she have developed the disability without any lesions in her central nervous system? Did she have genuine symptoms related to a dysfunctional central nervous system rather than MS itself? Had she become a prisoner of her subconscious mind, causing her to have a psychosomatic disorder?

Recent scientific evidence explains how the mind affects organic functions and that what happens to one's body may be linked to emotional stress. Changes do occur due to stress—some rapidly and others over time—in the immune, cardiovascular, hormonal, and autonomic systems, which in turn, can affect the functioning of the nervous system. In his classic book, *Anatomy of an Illness as Perceived by the Patient*, Norman Cousins observed the importance of this phenomenon: "The greatest force in the human body is the natural drive of the body to heal itself, but that force is not independent of the belief system. Everything begins with a belief." Did Sandra perceive an illness in her mind, which then appeared in her body?

Seven years ago, Sandra had gone to her internist with complaints of tingling and numbness in her right leg. Her examination was reported as normal, but because she was a young, Caucasian female, raised in the Midwest (where MS is common), the internist entertained the possibility of such a diagnosis and referred her to a neurologist. Sandra immediately read everything she could find about MS and became firmly convinced that, indeed, she had the disease. By the time she saw a neurologist six months later, she offered a classical history that fit all criteria for "clinically definite MS."

At that time, the diagnosis of MS was based solely on clinical history and physical findings; Sandra met all of the diagnostic criteria. Clinical history and careful examination still remain the basis of diagnosis of this disease, which is the most common cause of non-traumatic disability in young adults in the United States. Nevertheless, there is still no test to confirm a diagnosis of MS. While an MRI can be normal in the beginning, it almost always does become abnormal as the disease evolves.

"Sandra," I said. "I have very good news for you. You do not have MS. What you are suffering from is an energy block," I explained in the simplest way I could. She agreed to try to "undo the block" and to be videotaped before and after such a trial. Now, there is no scientific way to undo an "energy block." One has to talk compassionately with the patient, firmly implanting the thought in her subconscious mind that she will recover her normal, healthy state. I asked her to close her eyes and to visualize herself— first, reading a book and, then, walking across the exam room—as I gently massaged her neck to "unblock" the energy.

After a few minutes, I asked her to open her eyes. She could see me for the first time and was ecstatic. I gave her a magazine, which she could read. I coaxed her to get up from the chair and walk. At first, she was not sure, but with some encouragement, she did get up and walked the length of the room without any assistance.

I still love watching the video, which documents all of the above and ends with my receiving a huge hug from Sandra. I show it to other physicians and medical staff in training to emphasize the importance of listening to and observing a patient and only then performing a good clinical examination to arrive at a diagnosis.

"There is no more difficult art to acquire than the art of observation," wrote Sir William Osler. "The value of experience is not in seeing much, but in seeing wisely." Is this aspect of medical practice becoming extinct?

Physicians are now required to have a computer literally in front of their patients and spend more than half the precious time allowed for a patient visit on that computer. Eye contact is minimal. Observational time is nonexistent as they complete the template with patient symptoms and exam details. Vital signs are programmed to pop up on the template, yet doctors sometime do not even review them.

Is this the reason Sandra was not properly diagnosed by so many physicians she had visited over the years? Did they simply accept the diagnosis and then offer symptomatic relief for all of her problems, including bladder surgery to insert a catheter?

Abraham Verghese, professor for the Theory and Practice of Medicine at the Stanford University School of Medicine, senior associate chair of the Department of Internal Medicine, and author of three *New York Times* bestselling books, is a strong advocate of the value of bedside skills and the physical examination of a patient to arrive at a diagnosis. He firmly believes that the art of "listening to and examining the patient" is waning in an era of increasingly sophisticated medical technologies.

"Modern medicine is in danger of losing a powerful, old-fashioned tool: human touch," according to Verghese. In this new time of curtailed reimbursement for medical care and emerging digital-age medicine, doctors are required to behave like assembly-line workers. Patients become mere data points. Verghese calls them "iPatients." What is entered into the computer determines the type and number of investigations that must be done and eventually even tells the doctor what therapy is preapproved for that patient.

I was recently talking to a young physician who has been using EHR (electronic health records) for the past two years. He shared a very interesting story with me. It was a busy day in the clinic, and as was his habit, he opened up the patient's electronic chart to review before going to the examination room to see her. He reviewed her last clinic visit notes, her current medications, and her most recent laboratory results, which revealed that her blood glucose was running high.

He looked at the patient's current complaints of pains in her feet, which were well summarized by the nurse. He ordered a nerve conduction study to make sure the patient did not have a condition called neuropathy due to her diabetes. Then, he electronically prescribed an oral medicine for her leg discomfort and adjusted her diabetic medications on her electronic med sheet. When he finished with that chart, he opened the one belonging to the next patient.

An hour later, the patient with diabetes went to the nursing desk to ask why the doctor had not come to see her. It was only then that the young doctor realized that he had totally forgotten to see the patient! He had, in fact, treated the "iPatient," rather than the real patient.

* * * * *

Not too long ago, I was asked to see a young patient who had suffered a stroke while at work, resulting in a complete paralysis of her left upper extremity and weakness of her left leg. She had been flown to our hospital the previous day and had received the clot-busting anticoagulant called tissue plasminogen activator (t-PA). While IV t-PA remains the standard of care for patients seen within four and a half hours of stroke onset, outcomes are not guaranteed, and risks, including intra-cerebral bleed, are significant in about 6 percent of patients. When this happens, the fatality rate is 45 percent. There was no improvement in the stroke symptoms after she was administered IV t-PA. Diane was still paralyzed when I saw her.

The diagnosis seemed to be obvious. She was not moving her left side; the onset was sudden. Diane had had a "brain attack"—a stroke. It was a classic presentation, just as described in a medical textbook. However, as I started to obtain her history, observed the way she was moving her body, and then performed a clinical examination, I became convinced that Diane, just like Sandra, had become a prisoner of her subconscious mind.

A normal MRI of the brain—which by now should have been definitely abnormal—affirmed my diagnosis. I conveyed the good news to Diane and explained to her, just as I had to Sandra, about "unblocking the energy." She agreed to have herself videotaped before and after treatment.

Within a few minutes, Diane was able to raise her paralyzed arm and resist the significant force I was using to push her arm down. She could also walk across a room without assistance. Indeed, she had not suffered a stroke.

What happened to Diane reflects an increasing dependence on technology, as well as minimizing or skipping the actual examination of the patient. As soon as paramedics had arrived at the scene, they noted that Diane was not moving her left side. The diagnosis of "stroke" was radioed to the ER of the local hospital. The ER physician did a very quick exam before rushing her to the CT scanner to get a brain scan.

Since the brain scan was normal, she was considered an excellent candidate for t-PA, but only if she could get to our tertiary-care ER within three hours. As soon as she arrived in a Flight for Life helicopter, her exam, according to our ER doctor, was consistent with a "right hemispheric stroke," and she was given the powerful clot-dissolving medicine.

Judging from the detailed documentation on the computer from the time the paramedics first saw her to when she received the t-PA, it was obvious that very little time was actually spent with the patient by any of the medical staff.

* * * * *

On another occasion, I saw a patient in our hospital who was complaining of abdominal discomfort. I looked at the very detailed hourly history of his pain recorded on the computer by the nurse, as well as by the intern taking care of him. As I pulled up his shirt, I noticed a massively distended urinary bladder, which none of the medical workers had taken the time to observe.

New hospital guidelines require meticulous computer charting, which takes up a lot of nursing time, sometimes even at the expense of patient care. It is impossible for each nurse to care for the number of patients assigned, dispense medications on schedule, and still find the time to truly touch the patient.

Sandra suffered for seven years and Diane, fortunately, for much less time, but there are thousands of such patients who seek medical attention every day.

Just how common is this problem? A recent study performed at eight university-affiliated general practices in the Netherlands estimated that at least one out of six patients seen by a general practitioner has a somatoform disorder, a psychiatric condition that causes unexplained physical symptoms. Some research has reported the prevalence as high as 30 percent. This is both a major public health problem and a significant drain on our valuable medical resources.

In a study reported by the Harvard Medical School, patients with somatization had approximately twice the outpatient and inpatient medical-care utilization and annual medical-care costs of non-somatizing patients. When these findings were extrapolated to the national level, the study reported that an estimated $256 billion a year in medical-care costs are attributable to the incremental effect of somatization alone.

And the incidence of somatoform disorders are on the rise. Patients with such a disorder have physical symptoms for which there is no demonstrable organic cause. Careful observation, a good handle on the patient's medical and personal history, and a meticulous examination are crucial to recognizing and effectively treating such patients.

Sadly, a proper medical examination is becoming a lost art. Sometimes, the physical exam is skipped completely, as it was with my patient who had a distended bladder.

This is not an isolated event. A similar trend is being observed throughout the country. Human touch is being replaced by "sophisticated" tests and an ever-increasing indiscriminate use of computers for electronic health record (EHR) keeping.

The Health Information Technology for Economic and Clinical Health (HITECH) Act of 2009—signed into law as part of the "stimulus package"—represents the largest U.S. initiative to date that is designed to encourage widespread use of electronic health records. This stimulus bill, signed by President Obama in February 2009, includes $19 billion to help the healthcare industry change over to electronic health records (EHRs), with an additional $50 billion to be spent over the next ten years. It is projected that with a 90-percent EHR adoption rate, $77 billion would be saved. The system is supposed to provide efficient, coordinated, safe, and high-quality care. Important information about medications, including dosage, time for renewal, possible drug interactions, and all allergies is available at the fingertips of the physician using an EHR.

Of course, this is extremely important information. Yet, there are many reasons to be concerned about the system. The most important argument in favor of EHR has been the sharing of patients' medical records by different physicians. This works fine as long as healthcare providers are within the same organization. In addition, there are different EHR systems utilized in the healthcare industry that do not "talk" to each other. This makes it extremely difficult to render coordinated care. Almost all medical records are now digital and paperless, so the patient does not have any records for a doctor who sees him or her outside of that organization.

Most important, however, this system is rapidly eroding the art of practicing medicine, the cost of which in years to come will dwarf the benefits and the projected financial savings attributed to EHR. The distraction it causes in the exam room defeats the main purpose of its implementation in the first place.

Moreover, pressure on healthcare providers to use EHR is huge. Strict implementation of this system not only allows hospitals to receive significant financial rewards from the government, but hospitals can now invoice patients for every billable service. This brings additional revenue to hospitals. Doctors are further pressured by the government. Those who do not adapt to EHR by 2015 face 15 percent cuts in Medicare payments, in addition to an overall drastic cut that became effective in 2013.

Do the overall financial gains from using EHR justify the death of the time-honored physical exam as we care for our patients? Or can the system be adjusted so that the physicians can reap the benefit of EHR while continuing to enrich our clinical skills? If the current trend continues, the more than $250 billion we spend a year for somatoform disorders that cannot be diagnosed with any other test beyond human touch may get worse. The financial burden of many such diseases that require physicians to actually listen and observe in order to diagnose will dramatically escalate.

* * * * *

Recently, I was asked to see an 85-year-old man who, for six months, had suffered from bad headaches. He had undergone sophisticated tests, including MRI and MR angiography of his brain, all of which were normal. Narcotic drugs gave him temporary relief.

I pushed aside the computer that had been placed between the patient and me in the exam room and started to get a detailed history. It became very clear that his headaches started soon after his wife of sixty years had passed away six months ago. He was eating hardly any food, had lost weight, and had not had a single good night's rest since his wife died. They had no children. The cause of his headaches was obvious. He agreed to see a psychologist, who "cured" him of the headaches. None of the providers, each of whom had entered an extensive write-up on him in his EHR, had even mentioned the tragedy this man had suffered.

* * * * *

I do not fault the healthcare providers, for they are trapped in a system that is overly dependent on technology and leaves little time to spend with patients. The upside of EHR is that it is expected to produce great cost savings in the future. The downside is that physicians are losing touch with the human side of practicing medicine. They are forgetting how to listen and think through each patient's unique situation.

It pays to remember that technology is not an end in itself; it is a tool to help us become more effective in making informed diagnoses and decisions. The personal relationship between the doctor and the patient is extremely important and cannot be replaced by robotic machines. The power of touching and the effect it has on our patients cannot be measured.

We all know that when we are hurting, a simple touch or a hug does wonders. As physicians, we need to heal our patients. We need to touch our patients. In the current healthcare environment, payments to physicians are tied strictly to billable codes. Touching and emotionally connecting with patients has no acceptable billable code. Efforts are focused on what can be billed. Physicians are penalized by way of non-payment for failing to follow the pre-set guidelines, even if they sound ridiculously out of place as we care for our patients.

In her book, *Touch*, Dr. Tiffany Field, PhD, director of the Touch Research Institute at the University of Miami School of Medicine, discusses the importance of touch. Touch can help reduce pain, anxiety, depression, and aggressive behavior; promote immune function and healing; and lower heart rate and blood pressure. In a world of high-tech medicine, human touch and human concern are the most important qualities. If these are lost, it may take a long time to find them again.

The art of medicine is threatened by the changes underway in the healthcare system today. Rather than understanding the cause of depression or anxiety and focusing on non-pharmacological ways to treat these disorders, there is now an increasing reliance on psychotropic drugs. Perhaps the two main reasons for this trend are that physicians have limited time to spend with their patients, and patients are looking for quick fixes.

According to the Centers for Disease Control and Prevention (CDC), nearly half of all Americans now use prescription drugs on a regular basis and approximately one-third take two or more of them. Children in the United States are three times more likely to be prescribed antidepressants than those in rest of the world. In 2010, the average teen in this country was taking 1.2 central-nervous-system drugs—drugs that treat conditions such as ADHD and depression.

As a nation, we spent $2.8 trillion on healthcare in 2012. That's 18 percent of the U.S. Gross Domestic Product (GDP), making our nation's healthcare system the fifth-largest economy in the world. And yet, the delivery of healthcare in this country is gradually eroding. The solutions put in place to correct this problem are not working. Falling reimbursement rates and rising overhead costs force doctors to see more patients in less time to keep them financially stable. Allowing ten minutes per patient doesn't leave much time to adequately assess that person's symptoms or circumstances. As a result, the quality of care suffers.

The role of physicians at the center of healthcare is under assault. The confluence of economic and regulatory pressures is driving some physicians to early retirement and others out of the medical profession altogether. One-third (34 percent) of physicians plan to leave medicine within the next ten years, according to a report from the staffing company, Jackson Healthcare. Jackson's "2012 Medical Practice & Attitude Report" is based on several surveys of 2,000 U.S. physicians.

The following words of Sir William Osler are more relevant now than ever before:

> The practice of medicine is an art, not a trade; a calling, not a business; a calling in which your heart will be exercised equally with your head. Often, the best part of your work will have nothing to do with potions and powders, but with the exercise of an influence of the strong upon the weak, of the righteous upon the wicked, of the wise upon the foolish.

Physicians are fed up with the system and are sharing their frustration. However, those who attempt to organize are subject to antitrust regulation. By law, they cannot collectively fight the regulations imposed on them. Each doctor has to take on this fight alone. Rather than succumb to the pressures, some doctors are going back to practicing medicine the way they feel it should be practiced. They want to have a lasting and trusting relationship with their patients. Concierge or boutique medicine, as it has come to be known, allows physicians to practice their profession with fewer hassles.

This type of medical practice gives them time to truly know their patients and treat each one individually. This system of medicine allows a relationship between a patient and a physician, in which the patient pays an annual fee or retainer. In exchange for the retainer, doctors provide enhanced care, thus restoring the caring standards of medicine's past. The concierge practice is becoming more popular and is on the rise with an estimated national growth rate of 25 percent per year.

The greatest advantage of this form of practice is that it significantly decreases the number of patients per doctor, often reducing their practice to five to six hundred from the previous 1,500 to 2,000. This allows for longer appointments, better access, and individualized quality time with the doctors. These doctors are attempting to go back to their roots. They want to take control of their profession. They want to interact with patients rather than computers. They want to focus on real problems rather than on what is billable. Anti-trust regulations have for long silenced the voices of physicians, but the sails are already being filled with the wind of change. Let us hope, for the sake of the patients, that the ship reaches its destination before it is too late.

Enlighten the people generally, and tyranny and oppressions of body and mind will vanish like evil spirits at the dawn of day.
—Thomas Jefferson

5. EVIDENCE-BASED MEDICINE

Today we have a health insurance industry where the first and foremost goal is to maximize profits for shareholders and CEOs, not to cover patients who have fallen ill or to compensate doctors and hospitals for their services. It is an industry that is increasingly concentrated and where Americans are paying more to receive less.
—Dianne Feinstein

The European Committee for Treatment and Research in Multiple Sclerosis (ECTRIMS) holds the world's largest annual meeting dedicated to research in MS. More than seven thousand scientists and clinicians from around the globe attend this meeting. The 2007 meeting was held in Prague in the Czech Republic—the birthplace of Gerty Theresa Cori, whose landmark carbohydrate research not only led to the development of treatments for diabetes, but also earned her the 1947 Nobel Prize in Physiology of Medicine for science. Dr. Cori was the first American woman to win that prize.

The roots of the research paper I had submitted for presentation originated in that city, as well.

Exactly a century prior, scientific work by Jan Janský helped pave the way for the ABO blood group system, still widely used. Janský is also credited with helping to promote the use of blood donation and transfusions, which continue to play a vital role in medicine.

My paper proposed a beneficial therapeutic role of plasma exchange (PLEX) for a neurological condition called neuromyelitis optica (NMO). This is an inflammatory demyelinating disease that affects the optic nerve and spinal cord and carries a grave prognosis. The five-year survival rate is 68 percent in patients with the relapsing form of the disease; the prognosis is even worse for patients who fail to respond to corticosteroid therapy.

Along with my colleagues, I reported a significant and sustained improvement in six such patients who had failed to respond to steroids. However, of the more than one thousand papers submitted to ECTRIMS each year, only 70 percent are accepted. I was, therefore, quite pleased to receive a letter of acceptance. A few days prior to my departure for Prague, I received yet another letter from the organizers, informing me that my paper was one of ten being nominated by the organizing committee for an award.

There had been no effective treatment for patients with NMO until we presented evidence that PLEX therapy could make a difference to such patients. My coworkers and I were elated because this recognition might make it easier to get PLEX approved by medical insurance carriers. Up until that point, we had to spend an endless amount of time convincing and pleading with those carriers for approval of PLEX for NMO patients who remained severely disabled despite corticosteroid therapy.

* * * * *

I still choke up when I think of Mary, who had become quadriplegic due to NMO and, despite extensive conventional therapy, continued to worsen until PLEX was begun. Within a few weeks of being put on this therapy, she was able to walk without assistance and resumed her plans to get married, which had been postponed due to her illness. The video recording of her examinations before and after PLEX is very impressive. As she walked toward the video camera, she proudly proclaimed that her wish to walk down the aisle was about to come true!

Sadly, Mary's wish was not granted. Her insurance company, citing "evidence-based medicine guidelines," declared that PLEX was an "experimental therapy." Approval for the therapy, from which Mary had benefited, was denied. Her condition deteriorated, she again became quadriplegic, had to be put on a respirator, and eventually, passed away. Nothing we said could convince the insurance company to stray from their rigidly held view that accepted only evidence-based medicine. It was also frustrating to deal with insurance-company-hired doctors who knew nothing about the disease and had never treated anyone with PLEX. Sadly, this situation is the industry norm rather than an exception.

Another younger patient, Angela, was fortunate to have a better outcome. An NMO attack rendered her completely blind in both eyes and paralyzed in both legs. While she failed to respond to corticosteroids, her vision and strength improved significantly when she was treated with PLEX. She could then walk without assistance, her vision improved, she returned to school, and she continued to improve with ongoing PLEX therapy.

Angela's insurance company, also referring to evidence-based medicine guidelines, at first refused to pay for ongoing therapy. Angela relapsed. She became blind and bedridden and gained forty pounds due to extensive steroid use, which did not bring about any improvement. She also developed severe pressure sores.

After seven months of pleading and sending pre- and post-PLEX video examinations to her insurance company, we were finally given the approval to treat her with this therapy. Angela began to improve with PLEX therapy, and within six months, was walking without any assistance. Her steroid dose was reduced; she lost all of the excess weight she had gained. She has remained stable while on this therapy for the last thirteen years, but her eyesight did not improve. She remains legally blind.

My team and I were certain that recognition of this therapy by ECTRIMS would make it easier for future patients—patients like Mary and Angela—to receive this therapy.

* * * * *

enial of coverage of therapy is not uncommon. It happens all the time. In a nationally televised commercial sponsored by Health Care for America Now, a group that supported the Patient Protection and Affordable Care Act, the claim is made that insurance companies get wealthy by denying coverage for therapy whenever possible. According to a report by David I. Sackett and his co-authors, published in the *British Medical Journal* in 1996, the phrase "evidence-based medicine" was intended for "the conscientious, explicit, and judicious use of current best evidence in making decisions about the care of individual patients."

Insurance carriers, however, have redefined the term in a manner that justifies their denial of therapy whenever and however they deem fit, insisting that the concept of evidence-based medicine was "invented and embraced by the medical community." It is suggested in a report, supposedly written by America's health insurance companies, that in order to be profitable, it is important to deny at least 20 percent of treatments prescribed by doctors. (While there is no tangible proof of such a report, the majority of doctors would agree with the commercial's assertion.)

The National Nurses Organizing Committee (NNOC) disclosed that from 2002 through June 30, 2009, six of the largest insurers operating in California rejected 47.7 million—*22 percent*—of all claims. According to NNOC, during the first six months of 2009, PacifiCare denied 39.6 percent of claims; Cigna, 32.7 percent; HealthNet, 30 percent; Kaiser Permanente, 28.3 percent; Blue Cross, 27.9 percent; and Aetna, 6.4 percent.

While this report is obviously debated by the insurance industry, my own experience as a treating physician would support that finding. Physicians across the country would support it as well; so would my patients, Mary and Angela. They were not independently wealthy and, therefore, could not afford ongoing therapy. Those who can pay out of pocket sometimes risk the possibility of losing all of their assets.

According to a 2009 report in the *American Journal of Medicine*, nearly two-thirds, or 62 percent, of all bankruptcy filings in the United States in 2007 were due to illness or medical bills. Most of those who filed for bankruptcy that year were well-educated, owned homes, and were employed in middle-class occupations; 75 percent had health insurance.

About one thousand companies that collectively report revenues of more than $500 billion per year provide managed healthcare in the United States. Health insurance company CEOs earn from several hundred thousand to millions of dollars per year, while an increasing number of individuals struggle to afford basic healthcare. According to *Business Week*, the average CEO of a major health insurance company made forty-two times the average hourly worker's pay in 1980. By 1990, pay had almost doubled to eighty-five times that average pay. In 2000, the average CEO's salary reached an unbelievable *531 times* that of the average hourly worker.

Performance-based incentives and compensation linked to the overall financial success of the company are the driving forces behind a rigorous protocol that denies coverage in situations, even in cases where the treating doctor feels it is medically necessary. The ever-increasing take-home pay for those CEOs reflects in part the effectiveness and strict adherence to these policies.

* * * * *

While I was in Prague attending the ECTRIMS, I received an urgent email from my assistant. My patient, Maureen, a practicing psychologist, had complained of weakness and numbness in all of her extremities, and within a few days, was completely paralyzed in both legs. An MRI of her spine showed an extensive demyelinating lesion in her cervical and thoracic cord—a finding very much consistent with the diagnosis of NMO. This diagnosis was further confirmed by a blood test that had become available in ground-breaking research by a team of doctors at the Mayo Clinic in 1996.

Maureen was now bedridden. She could not sit up without support and needed help with feeding herself. She was rapidly deteriorating, despite being on high dose intravenous steroids. Encouraged by our own experience and that of others at the conference with whom I had interacted, I advised that Maureen be treated aggressively with PLEX. Upon my return home, I examined her and was pleasantly surprised at the progress she was making. Although she still remained bedridden, she was now moving her legs. This was a good sign. I was confident that with continued plasma exchange therapy, Maureen would be able to walk soon.

Then, we received an urgent notice from her insurance company indicating that it would no longer cover her therapies. For insurance companies, it is very easy to make such decisions. They never see the faces of patients who are suffering. On the other hand, doctors who see and talk to such patients and their families become emotionally involved and want to do everything possible to help them get better. I hear this all the time from other healthcare providers at conferences I attend. The doctors complain of their struggles dealing with insurance carriers on a daily basis and how much time and many resources they have to utilize to get even FDA-approved therapy for their patients.

* * * * *

As recently as 2013, my staff and I had an experience with an insurance company that exemplifies the problem the majority of doctors face regularly. Chase is a thirty-six-year-old man who was diagnosed with an autoimmune disease called myasthenia gravis (MG) about four years earlier. This disease causes significant generalized weakness; sometimes, even respiratory muscles are affected, requiring the patient to be placed on a respirator. In some patients, the disease can go into remission for many years.

Chase was essentially bedridden with impending respiratory crisis when his neurologist transferred him to our hospital—120 miles from his home—for further specialized care. An aggressive management with PLEX averted the respiratory crisis; Chase gradually began to improve. Four years later, while he was receiving maintenance PLEX once a month, he was doing extremely well. We had been able to reduce his immunosuppressive drugs, which can cause serious short- and long-term complications. He had returned to work after being off for three years, and fathered a son who is now two years old. The weaning process from PLEX therapy had been slow and deliberate, because Chase tended to become weaker just before his next treatment was due.

At that time, however, his insurance carrier determined that, according to "evidence-based medicine," Chase no longer required ongoing PLEX, even though it is a FDA approved therapy for MG. A peer-to-peer review was granted at my request. I had to be available when they called at a specified time, convenient to them. An emergency-medicine doctor employed by the insurance company, who confessed to me that his experience with MG was limited to the very short time that they were in the emergency room, felt very comfortable with the decision taken by the health insurance company. He stated unequivocally that Chase no longer required that therapy.

I gave him my background and my experience in caring for MG patients. I told him that I actively treated the largest number of MG patients in the state of Wisconsin, that I am on the Wisconsin MG Foundation's Medical Advisory Board, and that I was awarded an "Outstanding Physician Award" by the national MG Foundation in 2010.

To this industry-hired ER physician, however, none of that was relevant. When I made him aware of the fact that Chase did worsen just before his next scheduled PLEX was due, and that stopping the therapy would most likely be followed by a relapse, he requested that I send him all of Chase's medical records for him to review. This is when I realized—and confronted him—that he had made his decision *without even reviewing Chase's past medical records!*

This conversation was recorded by the insurance company in order to "improve the quality of care" provided to its clients. Recording of any telephone conversation by the insurance industry in such circumstances is quite customary.

As a result of the non-approval, Chase missed his scheduled therapy and, within three weeks, began to worsen. Double vision returned; he began to choke on liquids; he could not drive; he had to stop working; and, because of continued breathing difficulties, despite increasing his prednisone dose, his wife, Jessica, had to drive him to our ER, a two-and-a-half hour ride for them. She had to ask her neighbors to babysit for their two small children. Chase was admitted to the ICU and underwent several PLEX therapies. He improved and returned home, but was still not strong enough to return to work.

Once again citing "evidence-based medicine," the therapy was denied. (While PLEX is an internationally recognized therapy for MG, Chase's insurance company felt that PLEX should not be given on an ongoing basis, even though MG is a lifelong disease. This would be like telling a diabetic to stop taking insulin once his blood glucose is under control!) This led to another face-to-face, peer-reviewed appeal at a much higher level.

Jessica, Chase's wife, had to travel to another city for this meeting, leaving her sick husband and children at home. I, too, was forced to take time off from my clinic, not only to address my concerns, but also to answer their medical questions. Finally, I had to ask (and, yes, the meeting, as always, was being recorded for "quality purposes"), if they were denying my patient's therapy to save money for the company or because they felt that it was medically unnecessary. They were quick to say that it was not the money issue, to which I responded, "Then, it doesn't take a genius to recognize that he needs this therapy!"

There was silence. They did not address my concerns. They are driven to answer only to their shareholders and not to the treating physicians or patients. Their final answer was "no, the therapy will not be covered."

I was very much troubled by this. Chase was already on anti-cancer drugs and prednisone (which now caused him to have diabetes and excessive weight gain and necessitated insulin shots) and was allergic to the only other available therapy, intravenous immunoglobulin (IVIG). I called a senior neurologist at the Medical College of Wisconsin to independently evaluate Chase and to make appropriate recommendations.

Once again, Chase and his wife had to travel a long distance to be evaluated, leaving their two young children under the care of others. The recommendation from the neurologist who had been caring for patients with MG for more than thirty years was to resume PLEX as soon as possible. The insurance company finally approved only six therapies. What happens when his six approved therapies are over?

* * * * *

Chase's case is not unique. This occurs every day to many patients across the country. Insurance companies get away with these decisions without being held accountable for the medical outcomes. HMOs and health insurance companies are, for all practical purpose, immune to patients' lawsuits. They were the only industry exempt from such lawsuits until banks joined them in 2010 (in the wake of the recession). In 1987, insurance-industry lawyers were successful in convincing U.S. Supreme Court justices to have the federal Employee Retirement Income Security Act of 1974 (ERISA) put the industry above state common law, thus making it impossible to hold the industry accountable for its acts.

If a patient who is denied doctor-recommended care by his HMO tries to file a case in state court, where damages are available under state common law, HMO lawyers will have the case "removed" to federal court under ERISA's rules. HMOs or insurers that lose the federal ERISA grievance only pay the cost of the procedure or benefit they denied in the first place; no other damages or penalties.

What is fascinating is that the companies are required to provide the cost of the benefit only when the patient survives long enough to receive it. If the patient dies before receiving the treatment, the insurer or HMO pays nothing. Because there is no meaningful penalty for denying medically necessary treatment, there is no good reason to approve any therapy companies feel would be a financial drain.

In 1991, there was a well-publicized case involving Mrs. Phyllis Cannon, who died because her insurance company refused to pay for an approved bone marrow transplant therapy. Her insurance company invoked the ERISA ruling and, thereby, her husband received no compensation. The judges, however, were sympa-

Chase and his wife, Jessica, with the author in 2014.

Chase with his youngest son, when he was doing well with maintenance PLEX and before his insurance company would not authorize further treatments (2012).

Chase put on weight because of steroids (which did not help) and has developed diabetes because of it) while off PLEX. With resumption of PLEX, he has improved and returned to work full time as his steroid dose is gradually reduced (early 2014).

thetic and acknowledged the fact that the insurance company was clearly in the wrong for not approving the lifesaving therapy for Mrs. Cannon. But the law, they lamented, gave Mr. Cannon no remedy for his loss.

There is no remedy for my patients either. The appeals and peer-to-peer meetings are, for the most part, a farce. I have witnessed this first-hand. Treatment choices are governed by "clerks" or nurses who override the medical recommendations of treating physicians.

The agony and frustration at this gross injustice is well captured in a statement made by a woman named Florence B. Corcoran, whose full-term baby died in utero because her insurance company denied her appropriate and much-needed medical care: "If I go out on the street and murder a person, I am thrown in jail for murder and held accountable," said Ms. Corcoran. "What's the difference between me and this clerk thousands of miles away making a life decision that took the life of my baby? The difference is that she gets off scot-free and keeps her job!"

While politicians make abortion a central issue as they run for office, the powerful and rich health insurance industry prevents them from addressing the much-needed reforms that would hold the industry accountable for their wrongdoings. The industry also dictates what and when a particular FDA drug may be used. This is guided by the "kickbacks"—or "rebates" (as they like to call them, because that sounds civilized)—received from the drug manufacturers.

As a physician who specializes in caring for patients with MS, I marvel at the therapeutic advances made in the last two decades or that illness. We now have ten different FDA-approved therapies for these patients. However, the health insurance companies restrict our progress by approving only a select number of such therapies.

The selection of therapies is guided by "rebates received," according to a number of drug-industry officials I interviewed recently. It is well known that one year, an insurance company may designate a particular drug as "preferred" (Tier 1 on their formulary), only to drop it the following year in favor of another similar drug that had been declared "non-preferred" the previous year. There is no discernible reason for the switch, since there have been no new studies to show any difference in efficacy or side effects. The only difference is the amount of "kickback" received!

The trend now is for the insurance industry to engage independent "pharmacy business managers" (PBMs) as intermediaries to negotiate on their behalf. PBMs are driven by rebates. The higher the rebates, the greater the chances of a drug being approved and placed on the patient's drug formulary. It

takes a significant amount of time and valuable resources on the physician's part to convince insurance
company personnel that the prescribed non-
formulary drug is in the best interest of a particular
patient. Existing laws have made the practice of receiving "rebates" and restricting drug choices per-
fectly legal. It is also widespread and growing.

* * * * *

Maureen, my patient who suffered from NMO, was
getting worse. We needed to get PLEX approved
for her. A non-neurologist medical director, rep-
resenting the interests of a very large insurance company, refused to authorize the therapy. I requested
and received a call from a neurologist (hoping that he
or she would at least know about NMO), who bla-
tantly told me that he was calling me because he was
fulfilling his obligations, but no, he would not authorize therapy for Case Number XYZ. (In all my dealings
with insurance companies over the years, I have yet
to hear them mention patients by their names!) I
pleaded with him and gave him all the relevant published studies and data from our own recent presentation at the ECTRIMS meeting. It fell on deaf ears.
Finally, the industry-hired neurologist asked me a
question.

"Doctor, do you have a son"?

When I told him I did not, he said that he did and that his son was a Boy Scout who goes to his annual meeting at a park that is extremely large. "We are that big. Our office area is as large as the park; we cannot make an exception for one patient. I will not authorize any further therapies."

By that point, I was furious at his arrogance and total disregard for human life. I said to him, "Well, when you go home tonight and put a plate of food before your Boy Scout son, remember it is my bedridden patient who is paying for that," and I hung up.

I must have made a connection. His good side came through. What I said may have hit a nerve because he called me the following morning to authorize therapy for Maureen. Perhaps when he saw his son eating his dinner that evening, he must have visualized my patient lying in bed. Whatever his reason, Maureen made a remarkable recovery. Now in her sixth year of maintenance therapy, she can walk without assistance and has returned to work, part-time.

In 2010, the same insurance company once again cited evidence-based medicine to refuse her therapy and that of my other two NMO patients. One of the patients, Debra, was bedridden initially and had made a dramatic improvement with PLEX. She was able to return to work full-time at a law firm and could also put in additional hours of work in a department store over the weekends. While on maintenance therapy for more than eight years, her neurological examination had remained almost normal. When her therapy was denied and stopped, she relapsed and became wheelchair-bound again.

This time, rather than fighting the insurance company, I called a senior medical science writer for a daily newspaper. He interviewed all my patients and wrote a compassionate article, exposing the insurance company for making money off of patients by denying them lifesaving therapies. A few days before the article was to appear in the newspaper, the reporter, as a courtesy, informed the insurance company of his

Debra and the author in 2014. She was wheelchair-bound for several months because of a relapse while off therapy due to insurance denial in 2010.

With resumption of PLEX treatments, she improved immediately and continues to work full-time.

intention to publish the article. That same evening, I received a call from the insurance company's senior medical advisor, stating that an expedited review determined that the therapy for my patients was approved; it was no longer necessary for the article to appear in the newspaper. Upon receipt of a written statement that PLEX would be covered for NMO patients, I informed the reporter that the mission was accomplished, and therefore, it was not necessary to publish the article!

That evening, I wondered how many patients suffer because their physicians simply have no time or have "just given up" fighting insurance companies. Physicians are trained to heal, not to have to fight for what they believe is the right medical therapy for their patients. The health insurance industry *must* be held

Maureen with the author in April, 2014. She continues to do well and is able to get around using a cane.

accountable for its unethical behavior. Lawmakers and politicians have the means to correct the situation we are in now, but they don't because they are influenced by the significant financial backing they receive from the insurance industry. This has to change for any meaningful change to occur.

* * * * *

The United States leads the world in medical innovation. The ten most important medical discoveries in the first decade of this century occurred in this country, according to a large number of physicians surveyed throughout the world. Some of these include:

- Mapping the human genome in 2000. For the first time, the world could read the complete set of human genetic information and thus pave the way for medical therapeutic research related to genetic disorders

- Stem cell research: In 1998, James Thomson (University of Wisconsin–Madison) was the first to isolate and grow human embryonic stem cells in the lab. He helped discover a new way of creating stem cells in 2007 by reprogramming skin cells back to their embryonic state.

- Functional MRI (fMRI): A more focused version of MRI, fMRI allows researchers to map areas of the brain that they had no access to in the past.

- Laparoscopic and microsurgery: These procedures have reduced the risk for common surgeries significantly. Patients are up and running within a few days from surgeries that used to have a recovery time of a month or longer.

We have the best and the most recently discovered therapies available for many diseases. We have the latest medical technologies and innovations. All of this is possible because of the close and symbiotic relationship that has existed for hundreds of years between physicians, the pharmaceutical industry, government-sponsored research, and the bio-medical industry. This vital link of progress is now being gradually eroded by restrictions imposed on physicians by insurance companies, as well as by the government-approved mandatory guidelines, distancing physicians from the pharmaceutical industry.

The Physician Payments Sunshine Act, passed as part of the Patient Protection and Affordable Care Act, requires that as of August 1, 2013, manufacturers of pharmaceutical and medical devices begin to collect and document all payments over the amount of $10 made to physicians and teaching hospitals. This includes any and all forms of payment such as gifts, honoraria and awards, stock options, royalties, and research funding. If a reprint of a scientific paper from a peer-reviewed journal is provided to a physician, a value has to be attached to it and reported.

On the other hand, pharmaceutical companies have a product to sell and want their product to be the first that comes to mind when the doctor pulls out the prescription pad and pen, which may have the company's logo emblazoned on it. As a result of the Affordable Care Act, pharmaceutical companies can no longer give out such products to healthcare providers. This is ironic because these companies can still attempt to influence us to prescribe their drugs through ubiquitous advertising campaigns.

Recently, I was invited to give a talk at a prestigious university in California. After my presentation, residents and interns gathered around me to have an informal discussion. I knew exactly why one of the medical interns had an adhesive bandage wrapped around his pen, but I asked him anyway,

"Doctor, are you healing the pen?"

He smiled and said, "Not really. It is to hide the pharmaceutical company's logo. We are not supposed to be influenced by pharma. We cannot attend any lectures sponsored by the industry, and we are told not to talk to the pharmaceutical reps."

I smiled, but not at him. I smiled because, in the real world, it is the insurance companies who dictate what medicine your patient will or will not receive. I smiled because the honorarium I received for my talk was made possible by an unrestricted grant the university had received from a pharmaceutical company.

I smiled because it was otherwise painful to see how the university was preparing its students for the real world of medical practice. I was also saddened by the fact that rather than educating the doctors-in-training about how to critically analyze the drug-trial studies and intelligently deal with the pharmaceutical industry, the medical establishment would *rather throw out the baby with the bath water.*

Instead of confronting and appropriately dealing with the problem, universities across the country are simply shutting their doors to the pharmaceutical industry. In so doing, the universities and medical colleges are completely missing the point. In the real world, doctors will have to face pharma reps, but rather than training medical students to understand research, critically analyze the data, and ask the right questions, their solution is to cut out the pharmaceutical industry completely.

Doctors don't have enough time to read about all these clinical trials, which lead to more than twenty new drugs approved by FDA each year. They must learn to ask the right questions. This reminds me of the old Chinese proverb, "Give a man a fish and you feed him for a day; teach a man to fish and you feed him for a lifetime." It is more worthwhile to teach someone to do something than to do it for them!

There is no denying that drug companies spend millions of dollars marketing their products to physicians. In 1997, the FDA allowed them to market directly to consumers via public media, including television, newspapers, the Internet, and roadside billboards. In fact, in 2012, the US pharmaceutical industry spent $3.1 billion on advertising prescription drugs directly to consumers. Patients who first learn about these drugs from such media are encouraged to "Ask your doctor if you need [name of product]." It is not unusual for patients to shop around until they find a doctor who will prescribe what they want.

This form of marketing has become so effective that drug companies are now profiting by millions of dollars in the United States and New Zealand (the only two countries in the world in which this practice is legal). I wonder what is worse: letting pharma continue to interact with physicians to "educate" them on their products or having patients get their information from TV or other media and then seek out the therapy they want.

Those who favor direct advertising to consumers argue that these ads are truly educational. They inform patients about diseases and possible treatments. Sometimes, people suffer through problems and do nothing about them until they see their conditions acted out on TV and realize that there is an effective therapy. Ads more often encourage people to seek medical advice. Those against such ads argue that they misinform patients and promote drugs before long-term safety profiles can be known.

In addition, prescription drug advertising pressures health professionals into prescribing particular medications because patients want them. People want quick fixes; they don't worry about the potential long-term complications of drugs.

In 1997, as a result of direct pressure from the pharmaceutical industry and consumers, the FDA allowed direct-to-consumer (DTC) prescription drug ads on television and radio. The American Medical Association officially voiced its concerns and predicted the potential serious complications of this ruling by the FDA. Seventeen years after direct-to-consumer drug advertising was instituted in the United States, 70 percent of adults and 25 percent of children are on at least one prescription drug. According to a study conducted by the Congressional Budget Office in 2011, the average number of prescriptions for new drugs with DTC advertising is nine times greater than prescriptions for new drugs without DTC ads.

Internet access has also made it possible for patients to go prepared for their clinic visits and to have a dialogue with their doctors. Increasingly and rightfully so, they want to participate in their health-care choices. This is one of the reasons it is so vital to prepare future doctors to critically and intelligently interact with, rather than shielding them from, the pharmaceutical industry. It is equally important to prepare them to fight for what they believe is right for their patients.

Physicians spend four years in medical school and an additional four or more in their areas of specialization before they begin their careers. Fresh out in the trenches, in order to survive, they have to deal with hospital administrators, health insurance companies, pharmaceutical companies, and many other agencies.

For their sakes and for the sake of their patients, physicians cannot afford to be the weakest link in that chain.

6. SOMEDAY NEVER COMES

Begin now, not tomorrow, not the next week, but today, to seize the moment and make this day count. Remember, yesterday is gone and tomorrow may never come.
—Ellen Kreidman

Live as if you were to die tomorrow.
Learn as if you were to live forever.
—Mahatma Gandhi

Charles was the last patient on my list to see that evening. I kept it that way because I wanted to spend some extra time with his wife, Christiane, before she left to stay in the hospitality room provided by the hospital to get some rest. I walked over to the intensive care unit and checked Charles's progress on the computer. His electronic health record gave me all of his laboratory results. I reviewed the notes recorded by other caregivers and looked at his brain MRI, which had been performed earlier that afternoon.

Modern technology lets me access all this information in a very short time, but while the computer can tell me everything I need to know about a patient, it has yet to take over what a physician can do. A computer cannot touch a patient or look into his eyes to determine what is ailing him. A computer cannot feel the fear, sadness, or the anguish of patients or their loved ones. Holding patients' hands, or at times just simply listening to them, goes a long way in their healing process.

I entered Charles's room. Christiane was standing next to his bed, leaning over him slightly. Her left hand rested on his forehead, while she held his hand with her right. Charles was comatose and was being kept alive by a respirator. He had been admitted to the hospital a week ago because of chest pains and then had suffered a massive stroke. My brief neurological examination confirmed what others had noted in the chart for the past five days. There was no sign of improvement.

I put my arm around Christiane's shoulders and led her gently to a sofa so that we could talk. She had just turned seventy-six; Charles was eighty-two. They had been married for forty-two years. Charles was born in Boston and had settled in North Carolina with his wife, who was originally from France.

They were in town to celebrate their grandson's college graduation in Burlington, Wisconsin, a small town about thirty-six miles southwest of Milwaukee. It was during the dinner party that Charles had developed a transient difficulty with his speech and severe chest pains. The paramedics first rushed him to a local hospital and then immediately moved him to a larger hospital in Milwaukee to undergo an emergency coronary artery bypass surgery. He did well at first, but on the second day, he suffered a large stroke in the brain stem, an area of the brain that controls vital bodily functions, including consciousness.

Despite her age, Christiane refused to leave her husband's bedside, except for a few hours at night when she went to a room provided for her use in the hospital on the same floor as the ICU.

As we walked toward the sofa, many thoughts went through my mind. How do you begin to talk about an end-of-life situation with someone like Christiane? She had received daily updates and was fully aware that Charles had suffered extensive and an irreversible damage to his brain. Over the past several days, she had told me so many things they had done together and how much still remained to be done.

As she spoke, she kept her gaze fixed on Charles's face, never once looking up at me. She knew why I wanted to talk to her now. The few steps we took towards the sofa were probably the most difficult ones she had ever taken in her life. They were difficult for me as well. As we sat down, she looked at me, and I could see that her eyes were moist. Mine were, too. She searched my face to see if she could read my thoughts before she finally spoke.

"Doctor, as long as his heart is beating, I want Charles to be with me," she said. "It doesn't matter if he is on a respirator. I want to take him home. Every day with him is precious for me. There are so many things I want to tell him and share with him. Our forty-two years together went by so fast. It was like I blinked my eyes, and those years had just slipped away."

I promised to send in a social worker in the morning to arrange for Charles to be transferred to their home in North Carolina when he was medically stable enough to travel. After we had talked about what to expect as the days progressed, I got up to leave.

Christiane grabbed my hand in hers and said, "It is late in the evening. Go home to your family. As for me, I am going to spend the night here with Charles. It may be my last night with him." She hesitated for a moment and then said, "Remember, Doctor, someday never comes!"

Her words stopped me in my tracks! I had an epiphany. For the first time, I understood the true meaning of what she had just said to me. The twenty-minute ride home that evening forever changed the way I would lead my life. As I got out of the car and walked towards my house, I felt almost weightless with a sense of joyful lightness. In her darkest hours, Christiane had managed to light a fire of life in me!

I always maintain an ambitious list of things to do. However, I used to wait until the time was right, all the stars were well aligned, and conditions were just perfect before I would venture to achieve my tasks. As a result, it would take forever to accomplish my goals. I had read inspirational quotes like, "The best time to start was last year. The second best time is right now." However, none of the sayings had any lasting effect on me until I heard what Christiane had said to me so softly that evening.

"Remember, someday never comes."

Charles and Christiane in the ICU at St. Luke's Medical Center (Milwaukee, WI in 2007).

I had looked at Charles connected to the respirator and thought that might be the last time I would see him alive. He could be dead the following morning. And then I began to think about my own family and my goals and things I would like to achieve and the places I want to visit. What was I waiting for?

We take so many things for granted, including our own health. And time does fly by so fast, as Christiane had said. Before we know it, our bodies slow down, but the kid in us lives on and keeps on dreaming. Eventually, our dreams remain unrealized because we never act on them.

A simple but telling study conducted by Bronnie Ware, an Australian nurse who cared for patients in the last twelve weeks of their lives, is one that everyone should read and digest. Ware writes in her book, *The Top Five Regrets of the Dying*, that unfulfilled dreams were the commonest regret. This realization was painful for her patients because they died knowing that failure to fulfill their dreams was due to the choices they had made or not made. So, what prevented these patients from achieving their desires?

The commonest reason cited was that they had waited too long! They had waited for the "right time to do things" often until it was too late. In the last days of their lives, these people were passing on a powerful message to us. We all can learn from their regrets. Some derive inspiration from books and others from people like Christiane. For some, however, the realization does not sink in until an unforeseen, life-changing experience awakens the fire in them.

This was true for another one of my patients.

* * * * *

Anne (not her real name) kept dropping the percussion hammer as she examined her patient. This was highly unusual for her, but she didn't think much about it. It had been a busy day at the clinic, and this patient was her last one for the day. She blamed her clumsiness on being exhausted. A good night's rest would help, she thought. As she drove home that evening, she began to see double. This persisted even after she blinked a few times, and then she panicked. There was something wrong with her. She pulled over and called her husband, who is also a physician. I saw her in the emergency room that night. After a thorough clinical examination, I ordered some blood tests and MRI scans of the brain and cervical cord.

She outright rejected my recommendation to hospitalize her. She had three young children at home and wanted to be with them. As a physician, she fully recognized the importance of arriving at a diagnosis promptly, but as a patient, she was truly frightened as to what that diagnosis could be. That day, however, Anne had an overwhelming urge to be with her children. Her role as a mother overshadowed all her other priorities. She promised to see me in the clinic as soon as the MRI scans were completed the following day.

When Anne and her husband arrived, I placed the MRI pictures on the X-ray view box and outlined the abnormalities in the brain and spinal cord. Anne had Multiple Sclerosis. Tears welled up in her eyes. I am not sure how much she heard me as I talked about MS and the newer therapies that have helped improve the overall quality of life. I felt it was important that she start the MS preventive therapy as soon as possible and offered her a particular drug that was appropriate for her condition. I waited for her to respond.

The diagnosis of a progressive neurological disorder without a cure is hard for anyone to take. Anne had finished medical school when she was pregnant with her second child. The third one arrived soon after she had completed her residency training in family medicine and had taken a job with a large medical group. Her youngest was now three years old.

It takes a special person to finish a medical school and a residency program while caring for two young children and running a home. Anne's husband, an emergency room physician, kept an equally grueling schedule. They were now well settled in a beautiful house they had always dreamt of owning. Their student loans had just been paid off, and they were finally able to focus on their careers and raising their children. Traveling and going on exotic vacations had to be put off for now. There would be a lot of opportunities in the future to do the fun things they both desired.

True to its textbook description, MS struck Anne in the prime of her life. How does a person like Anne react to such a diagnosis? She had worked so hard to be a doctor, and just when things were going so well, she was handed a raw deal over which she had no control. She had always felt in control. Even when she was raising children and juggling medical school and a residency program, she managed well. Did she now fear that her career as a doctor was over? How soon before she could no longer be able to work? The first words Anne spoke caused me to shudder.

"I am worried about my children. They are so young. Last night when I went home, I knew there was something seriously wrong with me. I was very scared. Even though I am a physician and have witnessed death and diagnosed incurable diseases in my patients, it hit me for the first time that life is truly fragile. It was like some part of my brain just woke up! As I walked up to my children's bedrooms last night, I felt that my perception of life had changed completely. I began to appreciate what I have now, and it dawned on me that I may not be here to see my children grow up."

Anne had imagined a worse diagnosis. She expected it to be a cancerous brain tumor with a poor prognosis. She could deal with MS. She would fight the disease and overcome it, as she had all the other challenges in her life. That night, she actually started to "live."

It is remarkable how so many of us only begin to live when we recognize that death is inevitable.

* * * * *

Christiane recognized that and wanted to be with Charles. She wanted to be as close to him as possible, for she knew quite well that his body might not stay warm for too long. Each day with him was precious to her. As she wished, we were able to arrange for an air ambulance to take him to their home in North Carolina.

The next time I talked to her was seven years later. Charles had gone on to live for another four years. He did improve, but only slightly. He was able to get off the respirator and breathe on his own. He could not talk but was able to communicate slightly with his wife and caregivers. He received all his nourishment via a tube inserted into his stomach.

Christiane was by his side every day for four years, except for two nights when she left town to attend her brother-in-law's funeral. Although he remained bedridden, he never developed a pressure sore. Christiane checked on him every hour, even during the nighttime, to make sure that his oxygen cannula was in place and that he was comfortable. According to Christiane, he was never in pain. I asked her to describe the four years she spent with her.

"It was worth every second! I would do it again if I had to. I loved him so much that I could not just give permission to drug him enough, so that he could die.

Christiane and Charles in their younger days.

It ruined me financially, but I would have spent the last penny I had, caring for him."

Christiane had been forced to sell all their assets to pay for his medical care. Their farms in Wisconsin were the first to go at a much lower price than their fair market value because of recession. She now lives in a one-bedroom house, a far cry from the luxury she had been used to.

The hospice manager at one time consoled Christiane and asked her to talk to Charles and to let him know that it was okay for him to die. She must give him permission to die.

She protested. "How could I ask him to die? Just because he was not functioning by the standards set by the manager, should he be asked to die?"

Christiane loved him and cherished every moment she had with him. The experience was priceless. No amount of money could buy her the joy she felt when they were together. His death brought a dignified closure to her physical relationship with Charles. He died at home while in his sleep. He had shown no signs of any distress that day.

It was like any other day, except that their wire-haired dachshund called Cachou (named after French licorice lozenges, developed in 1880 by a pharmacist who wanted to help people gain a sense of fresh breath and health) kept whining and would not leave his bed. Christiane thought that the dog was sick and made an appointment with the veterinarian for 2:00 that afternoon. At 1:00, she left the room to get ready, and within five minutes, the dog stopped crying. She came back into the room to check and found Cachou licking Charles's eyes, trying to force them open. Charles had just passed away. Cachou stopped whining and did not need to be taken to the vet after all.

"Now," observed Christiane, "the pain of being lonely without Charles is far greater than my needing to sell off items from the storage to keep me going financially. You live your life only once. Do what you have to do, today. Listen to your heart. Do not wait for someday because someday may never come!"

7. PARALYZED

Obviously, because of my disability, I need assistance.
But I have always tried to overcome the limitations of my
condition and lead as full a life as possible.
I have traveled the world, from the Antarctic to zero gravity.
—Stephen Hawking

Some people are walking around with full use of their bodies
and they're more paralyzed than I am.
—Christopher Reeve

E ven though he had taken the Hippocratic oath
and firmly believed in its tenet, "Never do
harm," the palliative-care physician was completely puzzled by the answer he received from
his patient. Why did that patient want to live?

Gary was totally disabled. He couldn't breathe on
his own, had to be fed through a tube inserted into
his stomach, and had been totally paralyzed from below the neck for the past several years. He had no
control over his bowels or bladder. A tube inserted
into his bladder drained his urine into a bag and a
colostomy bag collected his stools. He suffered from
severe, painful muscle spasms in his legs, relieved
only by a continuous delivery of medicine into his spinal canal via a pump implanted in his abdominal

wall. A pressure sore in his back was deep enough to hold a fist. He had not walked in thirty years. If he had an itch, he was totally dependent on his caregivers to scratch it for him. And yet, he wanted to live!

A recent bout of MS had affected Gary's breathing, and he was now declared permanently respirator-dependent. Before the doctors could perform a tracheostomy, they wanted to be certain that Gary was in agreement with this plan of action. This was his chance to come off the respirator and "let nature take its course." In other words, he could choose to die.

It was thirty years ago when I first met Gary and took him on as my patient. I was training to be a neurologist at that time. Gary was diagnosed with MS at an early age, and by the time he was a teenager, he was already confined to a wheelchair. He was then forty-six years old. He loved cheeseburgers, French fries, and milkshakes, but had not been able to taste food in more than ten years. A permanent feeding tube was used for all his nourishment. He liked reading *Readers Digest*, especially its medical research updates section, and he would quiz me whenever he came for his checkups. But now, he could not read because MS had affected his eyes as well.

Over the years, I had witnessed a progressive decline, leading up to his present condition. Many times, I wondered what his life meant to him. How did he spend his days? What thoughts went through his mind? Being completely paralyzed and respirator dependent, what kept him "alive"? Did he feel sorry for himself when he saw people walking around and taking things for granted, while he had to rely totally on others for all his needs? Did he feel depressed? Did he pray every day and, if so, for what did he pray for? Did he keep on going because he felt there was a slight hope that a cure might come some day and make him better?

Gary had been confined to a wheelchair when he was in his late teens. His friends at the time were dating and engaging in active social lives. His hormones were also raging; so, how did he handle his sexuality then and now?

To seek answers to these questions, I conducted a series of videotaped interviews with Gary. What I learned from him gave me an immense respect for what we *have*, rather than what we *don't have*. "Live each day as if it is your last," was Gary's philosophy. He renewed for me the true meaning of "*someday never comes*"!

Just as I was trying to put Gary's thoughts and words on paper, I was deeply moved by an article that appeared in our local daily newspaper. It made me acutely aware of how physicians can sometimes totally block out of their minds what paralyzed patients like Gary must endure every hour of every day.

During a fifteen-minute clinic follow-up or a visit in the hospital, what they see and experience is the tip of the iceberg. The newspaper story described in great detail the plight of Dan.

* * * * *

In contrast to Gary, Dan wanted to die, but his doctors would not support his decision. Dan was twenty-eight years old, totally paralyzed from the neck down, and had been respirator-dependent since the age of three. A car accident had caused severe and irreversible damage to the spinal cord in his neck.

Dan can't remember life without a respirator. Even when he dreams, he sees himself as totally helpless and dependent on his caregivers for all his activities of daily living. It drives him insane when he has an itch and there is no one around to scratch it. His mother inserts a catheter through his penis several times a day to empty his bladder. He has no control over his bowels.

He can, however, see, talk, and take food by mouth. Most important, he can think, but thinking had become his worst enemy. He spends a lot of his time thinking about the state of his life—where his life is heading and the quality of his life. Is he a burden to his family? A few of the friends he grew up with are now busy with their own lives. They are married, have children, and are building their careers.

The only time Dan is able to get out of the house or escape from his "paralyzed state" is when he has appointments with his doctors, is on his computer, or is watching television. While surfing the Internet, even though he is physically in his room, his mind can wander out. Otherwise, he feels trapped in his body twenty-four hours a day, seven days a week.

There was no hope of recovery from his spinal-cord injury, which Dan knows very well. He is fully aware of the actor Christopher Reeve, who in 1995, became paralyzed from the neck down following a horseback-riding accident. Reeve had championed the efforts to find a therapy for spinal-cord injury without any measureable success. He died of cardiac arrest in 2004.

Reeve was married and had fathered three children by the time he became paralyzed. Dan, on the other hand, does not know what it is like to hold a woman in his arms. He has the same feelings and urges most people have, but he is paralyzed. He cannot act on his urges.

To get answers to my questions and to understand his plight, I called him, and he agreed to meet me at his home, a two-hour journey by car from Milwaukee.

The first time I visited Dan's home, I was struck by what I saw. His bedroom walls were covered with framed pictures of gorgeous young women, most of them in bikinis. Some of them were personally autographed for him by these women.

"I love women," he told me. "And yes, I did have sex a few times, but I never felt it to be real. It was meaningless to me. Emotionally, I felt so unsatisfied. There are times when I feel like a fish out of water, except that the fish at least has the "satisfaction" of thrashing its body around before it dies, whereas I can't even move a single muscle from below my neck."

He turned to me, and our eyes locked. His gaze pierced my heart and gave me shivers, the likes of which I had never before experienced. What could I tell a young man who cannot move any muscle in his arms or legs, one who is totally and permanently respirator-dependent, who requires catheterization several times a day to empty his bladder, and who is tormented day and night by thoughts and urges he can't act on?

The first words he uttered to me were, "I want to die."

How does one respond to that? Should I have shared with him my religious convictions and asked him to live out his life until "God" decides to let him die? Or, would it have been better not to invoke my personal beliefs, but to call on the words of renowned ethicist, Edmund Pellegrino, who said, "Doctors must *not* kill." Or maybe I should have reminded him of all the things he *was* able to do and admonish him to

Dan operating his computer using a mouth-stick (2014).

Dan with his mother, Cheryl (May 2014).

stop feeling sorry for himself? I could have offered him medications to treat his depression and wished that I did not have to see him again for at least six months, when he returned for a follow-up visit to the clinic. All such remedies had been tried on Dan over the years.

"I have been through all that," he told me. "Nothing has changed the quality of my life, and I do not anticipate any major breakthrough in my lifetime to make me better."

Dan denies any physical pain, but the emotional pain he feels is almost unbearable. Narcotics can relieve physical pain, but the emotional pain has been like a slow-growing cancer, getting worse as time progresses. "Sometimes, you can get rid of a cancer, but there is no hope of getting rid of that from which I suffer. I have lived with this pain for twenty-five years, and now I am entitled to eternal peace."

I questioned Dan's father, who had divorced his wife not too long after Dan had become paralyzed, but has continued to play a vital and a caring role in his son's life. I asked him why he did not support Dan's decision to die. Was it because he loved him so much that he could not bear to see him go, or was it his own strong religious beliefs? Without any hesitation, he answered that it was his faith.

Dan fully understands that some people have strong beliefs. He has had a long time to think about these issues. He respects the rights of others to believe in what they choose to be morally right, but he resents having those beliefs imposed on him. He feels strongly that, "Only someone is in a situation like mine should be allowed to make a choice between life or death."

* * * * *

Dan's situation brought to mind a very compassionate nun I took care of about fifteen years ago. I was working at a Catholic hospital at that time. Sister Mary was in her late sixties when she was diagnosed with amyotrophic lateral sclerosis (ALS) or "Lou Gehrig's Disease." Unfortunately, she had the strain of ALS that affects swallowing and speech early on and carries a grave prognosis. There is no cure for this disease. The end is painful. Patients literally "drown" in their saliva. Their chest muscles become too weak to initiate a cough response.

Some patients opt to go on a respirator and prolong their lives for varied amounts of time. Stephen Hawking who is a world-renowned theoretical physicist, cosmologist, and author of the best-selling *A Brief History of Time*, has ALS and has been severely disabled for many years. He was diagnosed at age twenty-one, and is now in his early seventies. Hawking is the longest surviving ALS patient on record.

I discussed all of this with Sister Mary, who knew very well what the disease would likely do to her. She had taken care of patients with a similar condition in the past. After a while, she took both my hands in hers, looked me in the eyes and said, "Doctor, will you take care of me when the time comes? Let me go peacefully? I do not want to go on a respirator, and I definitely do not want a feeding tube." I assured her that I would.

A few months later, Sister Mary walked into my office carrying a small suitcase and declared, "Doctor, I am ready to go. I have stopped taking all my nourishment for two days, and I am at peace. You promised that you would take care of me."

After examining her, it was I who now took her hands in mine and said, "Sister, you may be ready mentally, but physically, you are not ready to 'go.' When the time comes, I will be here for you!"

I ordered a meal for her from the hospital cafeteria and watched her eat; we both laughed afterwards! She passed away peacefully eight months later, just as she had wanted to.

* * * * *

What I learned from taking care of Sister Mary resonates to some extent with Dan's thinking. He felt very strongly that only those who had spent a week unable to move any extremity and were told that this condition would be permanent for the rest of their lives should have any say about his request to die.

"Only those who have been in my shoes should really judge me," he insisted.

Recognizing how well he articulated his feelings and thoughts, I asked him if he ever thought of being creative or of converting his emotional energy into something positive—becoming a writer or even a role model for severely disabled persons? As an example, I mentioned Stephen Hawking. He laughed out loud.

Yes, he had thought about it and had even obtained an associate's degree in criminal justice, but didn't have enough money to pursue this goal to the next level. He couldn't get a student loan. And even if he had succeeded, the amount of financial resources needed for him to be able to work would be phenomenal. Yes, he had thought about all of those things.

Just staying at home was costing him and his family a fortune. Medical and home care is expensive. His family has already incurred over $500,000 in debt. His motorized wheelchair was broken when I met him, and his insurance company had, thus far, refused to have it replaced. As a result, he had not been able to leave his room in several months.

With changes in healthcare, a time would surely come when he may have to move into a nursing home. This path would be far more economical for the insurance carrier. He had not had any pressure sores thus far because his mother and other caregivers take good care of him. If he enters a nursing home, he was not sure how long it would be before he developed a sore. I couldn't argue with him on this point because I have cared for many patients who are supported solely by government funds and their physical and emotional care is severely limited.

Yes, he had heard the questions I asked many a times.

"It is so easy to ask! No one ever thinks about what it takes to care for a quadriplegic who is respirator dependent—the amount of money needed to keep such a patient comfortable, to prevent pressure sores, for example. Besides, I am not a genius like Stephen Hawking, and I certainly do not have the money he has!

"But it is not all about money," he continued. "If I were to win a $50 million lottery, I still would not change my mind. I have lived my life, and now the emotional pain is a slow death for me. My mother, who has been my constant caregiver, has been with me every day for the last twenty-five years. She knows what I have been through. She supports my decision. I would give away my lottery winnings as a donation to any hospital, but only on one condition. They would have to agree to help me and others like me to die peacefully. I bet hospitals would then compete with each other to get my money," he said with a laugh.

My conversations with Dan took me in many directions. It raised important questions for which I have no answers, and yet, as a neurologist, I should be well prepared to face such challenges. To learn more, I interviewed eight of my patients, all of whom were paralyzed below the neck. All of them had become quadriplegic when they were adults, some even after they had children. But none was on a respirator.

* * * * *

The interviews for the most part were very emotional for my patients, their spouses (or their caregivers), and for me. They bared their souls to me. To some, this was cathartic and to their spouses, quite an eye-opener. The questions were not the routine ones physicians ask during a follow-up clinic visit.

Those I interviewed dwelled on their emotional and physical needs, as well as their frustrations and how it feels to be at the mercy of their caregivers. Most of their spouses or partners had assumed the role of primary caregivers and, in so doing, had stopped being "spouses" who provided emotional support. For them, the primary goal was to complete the daily routine and chores. The few hours they had between "shifts" were spent catching up with the other things they needed to do in and outside their homes.

As a consequence, being present when the interviews were conducted was heart-wrenching for them. Some of them broke down in tears. They had stopped thinking long ago about what their spouses were really going through all these years—what were they "really thinking"—as they cleaned them, fed them, and changed their diapers every day. How do patients react when they sense some resentment or frustration on the part of their spouses, while knowing full well that they are totally dependent for their care?

"This is very painful emotionally, and we suffer through it silently. We cry without tears!" was the answer that really pierced the heart of some of the spouses.

The family connection, the love of their spouses, children, and in some instances, their grandchildren, were the most common reasons cited for why they wanted to live. All but one patient lived at home. Their desire to live would be greatly diminished if they were in a nursing home was the unanimous response. While they did not want their lives to end, all of them indicated that it would be extremely difficult to want to live under those conditions.

They all looked forward to holidays, family get-togethers, birthdays, and anniversaries. Being loved and wanted and the warmth they received from their families was what made waking up each day so special. They all experienced depressive thoughts from time to time, but made a conscious effort not to dwell on them, immediately trying to replace them with the positive things they saw in their lives. They all seemed to have accepted their disabilities; they did not expect to get better in the future. They all said that moving forward was possible only after they had acknowledged that they would remain quadriplegic for the rest of their lives. Until that point, they had failed to recognize or appreciate the many things they could do with their mouths, tongues, eyes, and most importantly, their minds.

"Patience is absolutely vital to keeping your sanity," one patient told me. "You are dependent on others for all your bodily functions and needs. There are so many things I have learned to let go of. However much you want to get turned in bed, you endure the discomfort because you do not want to wake up your spouse or caregiver."

She continued, "Simple things like being covered with a blanket a certain way would be so much better; yet, you do not want to bother others because having your diaper changed and being fed and washed are far more important and take precedence over the 'simple things.' You endure the crease in the bed sheet and say nothing for the fear that you will be labeled as 'too demanding.' You learn to meditate and spend a lot of time thinking and stilling your mind. But thinking makes you smarter, while in turn, it also causes more pain, emotional pain. The world would be so much better if people spent more time thinking than talking!"

I shared Dan's story in detail with each of my patients and asked them what they would say to his request to die. They were all quadriplegic. Dan wanted to be judged by such people. All of them could relate to what he was going through; all of them were unanimous in their response: Dan should be allowed to die, if that was what he ultimately wanted. However, all of them made it very clear that their faith would keep them from entertaining such thoughts for themselves. That same faith, however, would also prevent them from judging others. Given a choice, they would not choose to die, but at the same time, they found it morally wrong to force their beliefs on someone else.

* * * * *

Gary eventually received a tracheostomy, and went home on a respirator. He was able to be weaned off the respirator, but continued to need the tracheostomy to clear secretions from his lungs. Six months later, he was transferred to a hospice-care facility, where he stayed for the last twelve months of his life. He was conscious and communicated with his loved ones until a few hours before he passed away. In the final analysis, nature *did* take its course—but not until Gary was ready!

I reconnected with Dan two years after I had first interviewed him. I found him sitting in his chair, connected to a respirator, with a stick in his mouth with which he was clicking away at the keypad of his computer. The walls of his bedroom had the same pictures of young, blonde, scantily dressed women. Nothing had changed in his immediate environment in the two years. I found everything exactly the same as when I had last visited him. It was as though the time had stood still for him. Nothing had changed as well. His wheelchair was still broken and awaiting insurance approval.

Whereas I had travelled abroad to Asia and Europe twice, flown domestically at least twice a month, driven ten thousand miles in my car, and moved my medical practice to a new location, Dan had rarely ventured out of his room in all this time. He stayed in his chair, unable to move any muscle below his neck.

When I asked him how he had been, he answered, "Same, Doc. No different, except my desire to die has become even stronger. I want to die. I want to put an end to my life. I do not desire anything else. Nothing interests me anymore. I used to enjoy watching television, especially the sports channel, but even that doesn't excite me anymore."

Dan spends about eight hours a day playing games on his computer. The rest of his time is spent sleeping, being nursed by his caregivers, and eating.

"The only thing I enjoy is eating. Death by starvation is not for me," he declared.

Seeing him surrounded by photos of beautiful young women, I asked him about his sexual desires. "I watch pornographic videos. I have a great imagination and sometimes I write erotic plays with me as the main character." He has never shared his plays with anyone. They are saved on his computer for his pleasure only. But it has been a long time since he had written a play.

When I told him about my other paralyzed patients, none of whom had wanted to die, he quickly pointed out that they had all lived normal lives before they became paralyzed.

"I do not remember my life without a respirator. I do not know what it feels like to scratch my face with my hands. I do not know what it is like to embrace anyone or to give someone a hug. I am trapped in my body, and the only way out for me is to die".

* * * * *

I have learned a lot from caring for my paralyzed patients, as well as from those I interviewed. It is not how physically disabled they are that matters. It is whether or not they feel there is a meaning to their lives. Being totally paralyzed is not a barrier to living a full, happy, positive life. Their minds are not paralyzed. In fact, they are more active in quadriplegics—and in some ways may work even better—than those who are not physically disabled. They spend more time meditating and thinking, which sharpens their minds.

Seeing someone briefly who is totally paralyzed and respirator-dependent invokes a response in all of us. "That patient would be better off dead" is not an uncommon comment I hear from healthcare providers. Some of them even declare that they would ask the doctors to "pull the plug" were they, themselves, ever to become paralyzed.

The palliative doctor who saw Gary could not believe that he wanted to live! And yet Gary had a wonderful eight months after he received his tracheostomy. Patients who have recently become paralyzed are easily swayed and tempted to end their lives. However, those who have had time to see and think through the options have are not quick to make end-of-life decisions.

* * * * *

What I have learned is that physicians should not assume that they know what is right for their patients. Supportive care and just being there, even if it means holding their hands and talking with them about their goals, no matter how simple, is sometimes the most powerful therapy we can offer. As physicians, we may not be able to help their physical beings, but healing and keeping their souls alive is important.

Now I much better understand the true meaning of what was stated more than two thousand years ago:

> ...*and do not fear those who kill the body but cannot kill the soul.*
> —Matthew 10:28 KJV

8. BREAKING THE SILENCE

When will we learn that human beings are of infinite value
because they have been created in the image of God,
and that it is a blasphemy to treat them as if they were
less than this and to do so ultimately recoils on those who do
this? In dehumanizing others, they are themselves
dehumanized. Perhaps oppression dehumanizes
the oppressor as much as, if not more than, the oppressed.
They need each other to become truly free, to become human."
—Archbishop Desmond Tutu
his Nobel Peace prize address, 1984

It was Friday afternoon, and just as I was getting ready to leave the hospital to go home, I was paged to see Paul. A young man in his early twenties, Paul had been hospitalized the day before for an emergency surgery for a burst appendix. That day, he was complaining of severe headaches, and his surgeon had requested a neurological evaluation. The CT scan of his brain done earlier that morning was normal, but since he had complained of chronic daily headaches and insomnia, the surgeon was obviously concerned.

I talked to Paul for a long time and then performed a detailed neurological examination, which was entirely normal. As I returned my medical instruments into the black leather bag and threw the stethoscope around my neck, Paul looked at me with tears in his eyes and said, "How I wish, if only once, I could hear my mother's voice. My heart still misses a beat when I hear my phone ring, hoping that it is she on the other end. It has been eight years since I last spoke to her, and I miss her!"

I didn't know how to respond. I was deeply touched by his sadness, but all I could say to comfort him was, "If the ties are strong enough, you will hear from her."

As I learned later, Paul was sixteen when he left home and moved to Milwaukee to attend a culinary school. Initially, he was good at staying in touch with his parents, but gradually, his letters home became shorter and further apart. He stopped answering their phone calls, and when he did answer, he knew he sounded distant and "lost in himself." His mother's Christian faith was strong, and because Paul assumed she would not accept him as he was, he simply pulled away. Finally, his mother was bothered enough by his silence to take the two-hundred-mile journey to be with her son and put things in order.

As a physician, I have been privileged to witness the most extraordinary energy mothers possess when it comes to caring for their sick or disabled children. I have seen spouses running away from the great sacrifices required to care for the chronically ill. But I have also seen children born with muscular dystrophy or other chronic illnesses whose mothers go to great lengths to give them as normal a childhood as possible. I know of grown-ups with disabilities who are shunned by their spouses, but never by their mothers. I often see aged parents wheeling their children to the clinic, and I marvel at the remarkable energy that somehow comes naturally to them when they are called upon to look after their children at any age.

As soon as Paul's mother saw her son walking toward his apartment, she stepped out of the car to greet him with a big smile on her face. He looked into her eyes, but did not return the smile. He wanted to say something, but was unsure how to begin.

Finally, he blurted out, "Mother, I have something to tell you."

"Let's get in the car," his mother replied. "Are you ill? Are you in trouble with the law? Do you need money?"

Paul slipped into the front seat, mentally formulating his answer. "No, Mother. It is nothing like that. It is about the way I am."

Paul's mother let go off his hand, cleared her throat, and said very firmly, "Well, then I know what it is; and if you think you cannot change it, you are wrong!"

"I wish you would understand." Paul tried again. "Being gay is not a choice; it is not a disease. I didn't ask for it. I was born this way. Please accept me for who I am."

Paul's mother was adamant. "No!" she insisted. "Come home. This city has been no good to you. You have been misguided. You will be back to your normal self once you are home."

Hoping to make her understand, Paul explained that he had been this way as far back as he could remember. Finally, in desperation, he rattled off names of important people in history who had been gay. "I do not want to come home," Paul repeated. "I am happy with who I am. It is you who have to change," he said as he stepped out of the car.

His mother tightened her grip on the steering wheel and, visibly shaking, turned to Paul and cried out, "May you burn in hell!" With those words she severed the strongest of all bonds—that between a mother and her child.

Paul's worst fears had been realized. He had lost his mother. It was an easy victory for ignorance and bigotry. He felt rejected, but yet, as he watched the car speed away, he also felt strangely liberated. The heaviness that had weighed him down for so long had disappeared.

Back in his room that evening, Paul looked at his parents' photo for a long time. Tears began to trickle down his cheeks. Now, he felt so empty, so lonely. He was only seventeen. How could he continue with his life when his own mother had shunned him? He glanced at the crucifix hanging on the wall and wished that he were blind or without a limb instead of being gay. At least, then, his mother might accept him, he thought.

Years went by with no contact between Paul and his mother. Paul cleaned homes in a wealthy neighborhood and was able to get a steady weekend job waiting tables at an upscale restaurant. He supported himself through school, and eventually became a chef at the same restaurant.

A year later during his routine follow-up visit at the clinic, Paul was somber and became teary-eyed when I asked him if everything was all right with him. He had just heard from his cousin, the only person in the family who had maintained ties with him, that his mother had passed away the day before from cancer. The last time he had seen her or spoken to her was when she left him standing alone on the street when he was seventeen.

"Doc, do you think I should go for the funeral?" he asked me. "I am afraid my family would ask me to leave, which would hurt me a lot. I have always loved my mother. I can understand why she rejected me. The entire country rejects us. The government treats us like second-class citizens, but yet has no problem taking taxes off our hard-earned money. Being gay is not easy."

Paul was angry. He was still hurting. He needed to be healed—not of being gay but of the pain of rejection and anger he carried with him. I did not know what to say at first, but after I had completed my clinical examination, I sat down and shared my thoughts with him.

"Paul, if you do not go for the funeral, you will regret it for the rest of your life. If you do go and the family acknowledges you, it could be a beginning process for you to heal."

Paul did go to the funeral. His father gave him a big hug, and they both cried. He reunited with his brother, who was now married and had three children. He met with his nephews and nieces and the rest of the family. His father, who is retired, now visits him periodically and stays with him at his home.

* * * * *

A few weeks after Paul's visit to the clinic, I was deeply disturbed by an article I read in *The Economist*. A horrific act of brutality had been committed on the west coast of Africa. It sent shivers down my spine to read about a young woman who had been brutally murdered in the country of Sierra Leone.

Freetown, the oldest and the largest city in Sierra Leone, had been founded in 1792 by freed American slaves, members of the Black Pioneers who had served in the British army during the American Revolution. Embroidered on their uniforms was the motto "Liberty to Slaves." After the Revolution, more than one thousand freed American slaves, including one belonging to General George Washington, the first President of the United States, set sail in fifteen ships from Nova Scotia towards West Africa. Sixty-nine of the former slaves perished on this "freedom voyage" before they reached the coast of Sierra Leone. There, the survivors of that voyage founded Freetown. Two hundred years later, the gruesome murder in this city stirred the moral conscience of ethically inclined people around the world.

Tuesday, September 28, 2004, was a sweltering day in Freetown. Fannyann Eddy, the mother of a nine-year-old son, was working late in her office that night. Except for the clicking of her typewriter and the gentle ticking noise of a rickety ceiling fan, it was quiet in the office. She was alone. Her staff had left a few hours earlier.

The world had taken notice of Fannyann after her impassioned speech six months earlier before the United Nations Commission on Human Rights in Geneva. She had implored the commission to take action against the oppressors of homosexuals in her country. She had dared to speak out against injustice perpetrated upon her fellow citizens—injustices that had the full support and encouragement of the newly formed government.

With the help of the British and a large United Nations peacekeeping mission, Sierra Leone had just emerged from a long civil war that had consumed tens of thousands of lives. The country was now liberated, and if one were to believe the speeches of its new leaders, Sierra Leone was about to be set on a progressive path.

Despite these intentions, violation and persecution of homosexuals had continued unabated. Fannyann had been encouraged by the change in power to speak out. Her speech had focused the world's attention on the serious human-rights violations being committed in her country. This had galvanized her to become a full-time activist. A framed photo of

Fannyann Viola Eddy (1974–2004) was an activist for lesbian and gay rights in her native Sierra Leone and throughout Africa.

Reverend Martin Luther King with the inscription, "Injustice anywhere is a threat to justice everywhere," hung on a wall facing her desk.

Late in the evening, while Fannyann was alone and working, a few young men broke into her office. They raped her, put a knife into her head, broke her neck, and left her to die. She was found dead in her office the following morning. The reason for this horrific crime was immediately apparent. Fannyann was killed because she was a lesbian. She was feared because she was an activist and spoke before an international community, seeking justice and to be treated with dignity.

Three days later, an equally gruesome act of violence was committed some four thousand miles east of Freetown—in a large town in Saudi Arabia where Islam was born. The event took place on a Friday, an important day of the week in Islam.

Hundreds of people had come to pray at the Grand Mosque. After prayers, most of them gathered at the central city plaza, notoriously called "Chop-Chop Square," eager to watch the weekly ritual of punishment meted out to prisoners. According to Islamic belief, Sharia law is an expression of Allah's will and is strictly but selectively adhered to in Saudi Arabia. There is no tolerance for any other views or religion in this country. In fact, it is forbidden by law to build a house of worship for any religion other than Islam.

As the van rolled into the center of the plaza, the crowd cheered. One by one, three young men in handcuffs, ranging in age from eighteen to twenty-six, were made to step out of the van. They all looked frightened. They searched the crowd, hoping to catch a glimpse of their family members. By this time, the crowd was in frenzy. It roared even louder as the young men were led toward the guards, who were waiting to put hoods over their heads. They were forced to kneel down with their heads bent forward.

Uttering the name of Allah, the merciful, and mustering as much strength as he could, a man in a white robe and a red-checkered head cloth lifted four feet of curved shining steel and with one forceful act brought it down on the neck of one young man, causing his head to fly off of his body and onto the granite floor.

Within minutes, three heads were lying in a pool of blood. Three young, headless bodies were now slumped on the polished granite floor with bright red blood spewing out of their necks. The underground drainage system, specially built for such occasions, sucked up the blood.

The executioner, looking proud of a job well done, wiped off the blade with a white piece of cloth, tossed it onto one of the lifeless bodies, and walked away with his head held high. His was a coveted job, often passed from father to son. He had to "kill" often, not only to maintain his skill, but also to keep his heart from wavering. If he didn't get to kill a human being, he was given a sheep to behead. He had done well that day. Justice, according to Sharia law, had been rendered by sacrificing these three young men because they were gay.

* * * * *

Paul in Milwaukee, Fannyann Eddy in Freetown, and the three young people in Saudi Arabia, all suffered painfully, as do countless others in the world. Not all of them are killed, of course, but many do suffer from the effects of unremitting stress.

Unlike other fatal diseases, emotional stress often causes a slow death involving great emotional pain, mental anguish, and feelings of hopelessness. Stress significantly increases the risk of cardiovascular disease, strokes, and cancer. Paul suffered for many years of chronic, daily headaches, and insomnia until he underwent extensive psychotherapy. Fannyann feared for her life, but continued to fight for justice and equality until she was killed.

The real question is who really murdered Fannyann? Who executed those young men? What caused Paul's mother to turn her back on her own son? Who should be brought to justice for these and other similar crimes committed on a regular basis throughout the world? Is it the society that fosters hatred as it did in Sierra Leone? Should the religious leaders of Saudi Arabia who preach hatred and dehumanization of those who practice a "forbidden lifestyle" be held accountable? Should politicians and leaders in our own country who not only fail to promote equality but also don't speak out against blatant discriminatory practices? And, finally, what about our actions—yours and mine—when we turn a blind eye to what is going on around us and silently tolerate discrimination? Do we not also bear responsibility?

Prejudice and intolerance are hardly new. The fight for equality and respect in the United States has shifted its focus over the years from civil rights to women's rights to disability rights to gay rights. The good news is that progress is being made, slowly but surely. In addition to the medical community, concerned citizens around the world are also beginning to address this issue.

In 1975, the American Psychological Association (APA) officially declared that homosexuality is not a health disorder. It took another six years before the World Health Organization removed homosexuality from its list of mental illnesses. The APA released a Statement on Homosexuality in 1994:

> *The research on homosexuality is very clear. Homosexuality is neither mental illness nor moral depravity. It is simply the way a minority*

of our population expresses human love and sexuality. Study after study documents the mental health of gay men and lesbians. Gay men and lesbians function just as well as heterosexuals do in the area of judgment, stability, reliability, and social and vocational adaptiveness.

Homosexuality is not a matter of individual choice. Research suggests that the homosexual orientation is in place very early in the life cycle, possibly even before birth. It is found in about ten percent of the population, a figure that is surprisingly constant across cultures, irrespective of the different moral values and standards of a particular culture.

Contrary to what some imply, the incidence of homosexuality in a population does not appear to change with new moral codes or social mores. Research findings suggest that efforts to repair homosexuals are nothing more than social prejudice garbed in psychological accouterment.

An increasing number of states are now banning "reparative therapy" to convert gays to straight. The American Medical Association (AMA) released a report in 1994 that called for "nonjudgmental recognition of sexual orientation by physicians." The report suggested that psychotherapy be directed to help homosexuals "become comfortable with their sexual orientation."

The nation, however, continues to pay a heavy toll for its intolerant policies towards homosexuality. Numerous studies have shown a higher rate of suicide attempts among gays, which is the third leading cause of death for fifteen to twenty-four-year-old lesbian, gay, bisexual, and transgender (LGBT) youth. They attempt suicide up to four times more often than their heterosexual peers.

This is true in the rest of the world as well. According to a study in Taiwan, one in five or 20 percent of Taiwanese gay people have attempted suicide. Approximately 25 percent of LBGT students are harassed because of their sexual orientation. Seventy-eight percent of gay (or believed-to-be-gay) teens are teased or bullied in their schools and communities, a percentage significantly higher than that of heterosexual adolescents.

Bullying and harassment lead to negative effects on the development and mental health of students. These behaviors cause extreme anxiety and depression, relationship problems, low self-esteem, substance abuse, and thoughts of suicide. LBGT students are also at much greater risk of physical assault than other children and teenagers.

* * * * *

The medical profession should strive to improve the health, safety, and wellbeing of LGBT individuals. Understanding LGBT health starts with understanding the history of oppression and discrimination that these communities have faced and continue to face. Presently in the United States, people face serious discrimination in employment. They can be fired, denied a promotion, and subjected to harassment at work; there is no federal law in place to protect them.

As Russia prepared to host the 2014 Winter Olympics, it came under considerable criticism from human rights advocacy groups for its strong homophobic policies and sentiments. In Nigeria—known as "the Giant of Africa" and the most populous country in West Africa with over 170 million people—in 2014, the president signed a law that bans gay marriage, public displays of homosexual relationships, and belonging to homosexual groups. Homosexuality is now punishable for up to fourteen years in jail in Nigeria.

Violation of human rights laws is on the rise in many African countries. Same-sex acts are declared illegal in thirty sub-Saharan countries and punishable by imprisonment or even death. In India, the world's largest democracy, LGBT people face danger of being imprisoned for life because of their sexual orientation. This law, crafted by the colonials in 1860, was upheld by the Indian Supreme Court in 2013.

In some countries, however, laws to protect and ensure equality are slowly being passed. In the meantime, those who have suffered or continue to suffer need to be emotionally healed. This is possible, as it was for my patient, Paul. It took a long time to overcome his somatic, stress-related complaints, but eventually he did heal. Acceptance by his family was a crucial element of Paul's healing process.

The initial reaction for many parents when their children reveal their sexual identity is one of shock. They are overcome with anger, grief, disappointment, shame, anguish, and guilt. For the most part, they internalize the problem and fail to focus on their children. They make it all about themselves instead of about their son or daughter and do not comprehend how much courage and anxiety it must have taken for these young people to reveal their sexuality. They fail to recognize how vulnerable their children are or how desperately they need their parents' love and support.

Until they are able to express unconditional love and compassion for their children, parents cannot begin to feel the pain. Being loved and wanted is a powerful medicine that can heal what modern medical practices cannot. It took Paul more than a decade to heal. He regrets that he never had closure with his mother or heard her voice again. His father, however, finally came to grips with his own fears and extended his unconditional love to Paul. The warmth of his hug is what finally healed Paul. Love is powerful.

I am reminded of Golda Meir's statement to the National Press Club in Washington in 1957: "Peace will come when the Arabs love their children more than they hate us."

I believe that healing will come when people around the world love their children more than they fear and misunderstand homosexuality.

9. PAIN

Give me life, give me pain, give me myself again.
—Tori Amos

In all that people can individually do as well for themselves, government ought not to interfere.
—Abraham Lincoln

D r. Bruce Smith dreaded going before the Pain Review Board, whose members had been handpicked and hastily assembled by the hospital administrators. There was a lot at stake. The Joint Commission on Accreditation of Healthcare Organizations (JCAHO) was due to visit the hospital in three months. Government-funded healthcare programs, which contributed to more than two-thirds of the hospital's revenue, would be adversely affected if the hospital failed to receive the coveted JCAHO's seal of approval.

More than 20,000 healthcare facilities are certified every three years by this non-profit organization, and the government has come to recognize JCAHO's approval as a condition for licensure and financial reimbursement. The preparation for the visit is a major undertaking, and the entire hospital is consumed by the so-called "Jay-co fever"! Everyone is on edge. Administrators run from one meeting to another; frequent mock drills are held for every conceivable scenario to ensure that all goes well in the final week. But now, Dr. Smith had thrown a wrench in the works, and this had to be dealt with swiftly, before JCAHO's arrival.

Armed with the knowledge that nearly one-third of Americans will experience chronic pain at some point in their lives, and that 20 percent suffer from pain on a daily basis, Congress felt compelled to act. It could not bear the fact that "pain" was costing the country over $125 billion a year. It went to work and expeditiously named the 2000s as the "Decade of Pain Control and Research." This bill, championed by the U.S. senator from Utah, Orrin G. Hatch, was passed by the 106th U.S. Congress and signed into law by President Clinton. The Pain Relief Promotion Act encouraged practitioners to prescribe and administer controlled substances to relieve pain and discomfort. In fact, practitioners were encouraged to treat pain aggressively even when the treatment might increase the risk of death.

However, even before the government made it a criminal offense to under-treat pain, JCAHO declared that it was the right of every patient to have his or her pain assessed, treated, and monitored without being influenced by that individual's social, economic, or cultural background. Any facilities that failed to follow these requirements risked their accreditation. Pain was declared to be the "fifth vital sign," along with pulse, blood pressure, temperature, and respiratory rate. For too long, Americans had suffered pain silently, but no more! The politicians had come to their rescue, and "the doctors, who for centuries had failed to treat pain adequately," would be penalized, as would the hospitals that employed them. Americans needed to be pain free!

"A patient is always right," declared JCAHO. A self-reported level of pain on a scale ranging from 0-10 was considered to be the most reliable indicator of pain intensity. Healthcare providers were now told not to rely on the patient's facial expression or body language to gauge pain management. A report of "severe pain" on the scale had to be treated, regardless of the patient's clinical examination.

Dr. Smith had been summoned because he had deemed it inappropriate to give narcotics to control pain in a patient with impending respiratory failure. With a busy practice and the respect of his patients and peers, the ad hoc board's decision to have him undergo mandatory classes to "learn how to adequately treat pain" hit Dr. Smith like a ton of bricks! He had wanted to be a doctor ever since he was a kid, to help people and alleviate pain and suffering. He had just finished paying back the money he had borrowed to pave his way through the grueling years in medical school, followed by four years of residency training. But now, that seemed to count for little in the eyes of the Board. Even the hospital's medical staff was aghast! Were they really under-treating pain?

If the few reports that had been circulated were correct, then up to three-quarters of all hospitalized patients suffered from undertreated pain. This surely was an eye-opener for the physicians. They were aware of the policy the Federation of State Medical Boards had issued in 1998, reassuring doctors that they wouldn't face regulatory action for prescribing even large amounts of narcotics, as long as it was in the course of medical treatment. But now, the government had made it very clear that under-treatment of pain was a punishable crime.

Dr. Smith was fortunate. He only had to be "taught how to treat pain," rather than being prosecuted in a court of law. The hospital felt satisfied with its action, as well. This is exactly what JCAHO was looking for. Disciplining a high-profile physician would send the much-needed message to other physicians who dared to let their patients suffer in pain.

* * * * *

What happened to Dr. Smith was not unique by any means. Similar instances were occurring on a daily basis throughout the country. Nurses were encouraged to report to the hospital administrators if they felt doctors were not prescribing enough pain medication. In fact, it was a nurse who had reported Dr. Smith after he refused to give narcotics to a patient for whom he had cared for years and was now concerned about her respiratory function. Narcotics would further suppress her breathing, Dr. Smith reasoned.

Doctors who failed to prescribe enough narcotics to control pain were now called "narcophobic." Articles in peer-reviewed nursing journals would define in great detail the characteristics of one who suffers from "narcophobia" and how to cure this "disease." Little by little, physicians began to see that a systematic control over how and when and with what they could treat patients would become the industry norm in the years to come. But they surely did not predict that this "direct intervention by regulatory agencies" would also lead to some catastrophic results, the magnitude of which this country had never seen.

"The decade of pain" that Congress had so ceremoniously ushered in ten years ago was a "great success"! The use of painkillers quadrupled between 1999 and 2010. Doctors now write about 300 million prescriptions a year for painkillers. That is enough for every adult American to be medicated around the clock for a month, according to the Centers for Disease Control and Prevention. For those patients who indicate the level of pain being high on the "pain scale," stronger pills are made available.

This mandate became a marketing opportunity for the opioid pharmaceutical industry. Prescriptions for potent painkillers increased by 52 percent over the last five years. In 2009, Purdue Pharma's Oxycontin, an opioid pain reliever chemically close to heroin, reached annual sales that topped $3 billion. That represents a 300 percent increase in annual sales in 2001. The United States makes up 5 percent of the world's population but consumes 80 percent of the world's opioids and, by some accounts, 99 percent of the world's Vicodin, a potent narcotic. Hydrocodone has become the most commonly prescribed drug in the U.S., more than antibiotics and cholesterol medications combined!

The 1999 law that "No disciplinary action will be taken against a practitioner based solely on the quantity and/or frequency of opiates prescribed," accompanied by other laws to persecute doctors for under-treating pain, resulted in a dramatic increase in prescriptions.

"Since the law changed, the average daily dose in morphine equivalents has gone through the roof," said Dr. Gary Franklin, Washington State's Medical Director for its Department of Labor & Industries.

For JCAHO and the politicians who championed a "pain-free America," this was a resounding victory, but it came with a most disastrous outcome. Alarming statistics are emerging. Prescription drugs now kill more people than motor vehicle accidents kill in this country. The number of deaths from prescription painkillers increased from 4,030 in 1999 to 16,651 in 2010. According to Dr. Thomas Frieden, Director of the Centers for Disease Control and Prevention (CDC), 125,000 lives were lost in the last ten years to legal drugs like Vicodin, Oxycontin, and methadone. Visits to hospital emergency departments that involved nonmedical use of prescription narcotic pain relievers have more than doubled, rising 111 percent between 2004 and 2008. According to the CDC, the incidents of teen fatalities related to drug poisonings among fifteen- to nineteen-year-olds increased more than 90 per cent between 2000 and 2009. The CDC's report states that this is a result of our country's epidemic of prescription drug abuse.

Every day, deaths from drug overdose outnumber gun deaths. In the United States, there are approximately 82 gun deaths and 102 drug-related deaths every day. It has been estimated that Americans are 6,200 percent more likely to die from prescription painkillers than by a random shooter! However, these statistics pale before the greater impact the "liberalization" of pain meds has done to the society as a whole. The number of drug addicts is at an historic high, and as a direct result, the crime rate has escalated, sexually transmitted diseases are on the rise, and prisons are beyond overcrowded.

According to CDC director Tom Frieden, while most things are getting better in the world of health, this situation is getting worse! Killing pain is what the Congress set out to do, but now the same weapon is not only killing people, but has profound and far-reaching consequences. The pendulum is now swinging the other way.

The U.S Centers for Disease Control and Prevention have declared prescription drug abuse an epidemic. A federal study released in 2013 found a 400 percent rise in overdose deaths of women from prescription narcotics from 1999 to 2010. The deaths from narcotics in New York City jumped 65 percent from 2005 to 2011. Hospitals across the country are inundated by addicts, whom they cannot care for because of lack of resources.

Lawmakers now are eager to take steps to correct the problem. The government is waging an aggressive war against pain doctors, making them the scapegoats for the failed drug war. Physicians present a better target than underground, black-market drug dealers. Today, though figures vary, many more physicians are convicted and in jail in the USA because of narcotic over prescription than ever before. Conviction of physicians across the country is beginning to have the desired and a chilling effect—as intended by the lawmakers—on healthcare providers. Physicians who prescribe narcotics are now being subjected to new laws, requiring them to perform certain protocols or face licensure actions—or even criminal prosecution.

These new laws are time consuming. In addition to performing a detailed history and physical, physicians are required to review mental health, opiate-addiction risk, and pain-assessment questionnaires filled out by patients. They need to discuss with patients the benefits and risks of opioid use, alternative treatments and medications, and counsel women between the ages of 14 and 55 about the risks of opioid use during pregnancy. An individualized treatment plan with meaningful goals needs to be developed and reviewed at every visit. Physicians are required to have patients sign a Controlled Substance Agreement that includes prescribing policies, consent to drug screening, permission to conduct random pill counts, requirements to take the medications only as prescribed, and the consequences of violating the contract conditions.

Additionally, physicians must order annual urine drug screening, review reports documenting narcotic prescriptions dispensed from pharmacies and see patients in clinic at least four times a year. As a consequence, some physicians are now under-treating pain or all together stopped prescribing narcotics. Medical students are discouraged from going into pain medicine specialty training. While physicians are being taken on a roller-coaster ride, it is the patients who suffer the most.

* * * * *

I recently interviewed Dr. Smith, almost twelve years after he had been summoned before the board.

"I treat pain, and I certainly prescribe narcotics," he told me, "but not based on any arbitrary rules and regulations handed over to me by some non-medical agencies. I honor the oath I took: to do no harm," Smith said. "And these medications do harm. You're free to practice medicine however you want. But you're not free to do things that hurt people."

His wisdom, which I have come to admire, is illustrated by a personal experience he shared with me. A few years ago, he was taking care of a woman with widespread metastases from renal cell carcinoma. She only had a few days to live. She was in pain. Dr. Smith made sure that she was being treated adequately but not to the extent that she was "knocked out," as the nurses and palliative care physicians had advocated. The dose they were recommending would surely "kill this woman in a few hours," Smith said. He was criticized for not heeding their advice and was called a "narcophobic."

It was during this time that the woman first came out to her family about her sexual orientation. She was a lesbian, and she wanted her parents and daughter to know. The family was distraught. At first, they could not accept what she had told them, but realizing that she was dying, they wanted her to go in peace. They met and recognized her longtime companion, allowing her to participate in the patient's final rites.

Dr. Smith pulled out a card he had received from the woman's daughter, almost ten years after her mother had passed away. In it, she thanked him for not "drugging her mother" in the last days of her life, because to her, that was the most precious time she had ever spent with her. It also allowed her mother to bare her soul to her family and depart in peace.

We need doctors like Dr. Smith to restore and heal the country. A finger on the pulse is far more effective than what an entire Congress can do to bring this country from the destructive path it was set upon more than a decade ago.

10. BEING IN THE ZONE

A man is but the product of his thoughts.
What he thinks, he becomes.
—Mahatma Gandhi

Positive thinking will let you do everything
better than negative thinking will.
—Zig Ziglar

We are what we think.
All that we are arises with our thoughts.
With our thoughts, we make our world.
—Buddha

The story you are about to read will forever make you pause and think about how to achieve your goals in life. It may even cause you to critically analyze the reasoning behind your failures and successes.

It happened fifty-five years ago in a small village in Kenya. Electricity had not yet reached the village. The road to the capitol city of Nairobi was narrow and made of mud. Grass grew in the middle of the road where there was no traffic. It took ninety minutes to travel a stretch of forty miles. Giraffes, zebras, and antelopes could be seen grazing the plains on either side of the road.

Sometimes, we would see lions and cheetahs. Occasionally, the road would be blocked by an elephant that would hold us captive in our car for a very long time. But the intermittent trips to the capitol were magical. As kids, we would marvel at how a flip of a switch could light up the whole room, and having never seen a radio before, we wondered how a small box could emit a human voice and music simply by turning a dial.

I was five years old then. I am not sure what inspired me, but I started to dream of becoming a physician. I had no idea what it took to be a doctor, but I knew I wanted to be one. My father and his younger brother owned a general store in our village. To make sure all of their eight kids stayed out of trouble during the weekends, they made us do some small chores in the shop.

My favorite task was breaking down huge bundles of old newspapers my father got from the city into smaller bundles and tie them up with a firm string made of sisal. The local vendors bought these bundles to wrap up anything that needed to be bagged. The usual brown paper bags were too expensive; plastic had yet to invade Kenya.

The newspapers originally came from England, and sometimes, I would come across pictures of a doctor performing surgery. I saved them and studied them carefully. If I was lucky, I sometimes saw colored photos that depicted surgery being performed step by step. After a while, I considered myself to be an expert and asked the workers at my dad's soda factory to lie down during their lunch break so that I could perform fake surgeries on them. And I had yet to even start grade school!

My ambition to become a doctor never wavered. I stayed focused, and soon after I finished high school in the city (our village did not have a high school), I was able to convince my parents to let me undertake a three-thousand-mile journey to India to pursue a medical education. I was sixteen at the time, and as I look back, I am quite convinced that some supernatural forces were gently pushing me in the right direction. I have come to realize, after having read many books on the power of positive thinking and the subconscious mind, that this is exactly what was happening.

* * * * *

The subconscious mind is powerful. According to William James (1842-1910, the father of American psychology), the power to move the world is in our subconscious minds! We are just beginning to understand the extremely complex physiological workings of the brain, and like the universe, the power of the brain has no boundaries.

A single nerve cell (neuron) in the brain is a very tiny cell, only 0.0001 inch in diameter. There are ten billion neurons in the brain. Each neuron has DNA with enough information to fill one thousand books of six hundred pages each. The human brain weighs only three pounds, yet in a life span of seventy-five years, it works 24/7 for a total of 657,000 hours.

According to the distinguished neuroscientist and Nobel Prize winner Sir John Eccles (1903-1997), who spent the last years of his life studying and publishing on the brain-mind connection, the human brain is only 10 percent functional at any given time. The potential of the human brain is infinite, he concluded. He also believed, "There is a Divine providence operating over and above the materialist happening of biological evolution."

Two years before I started medical school, I was fascinated by the news from South Africa of the first human-to-human heart transplant performed by Dr. Christiaan Barnard on Louis Washkansky, a fifty-four-year-old grocer. Dr. Barnard was assisted by his brother, Marius Barnard, and a team of thirty other people. I saved all of the newspaper articles and read everything I could find on Dr. Barnard. I still have those clippings. He became my hero and inspired me to push myself even harder to secure a seat in medical school.

Thirty thousand students were competing for six hundred medical college seats in Mumbai that year. There was only one way for me to secure a seat: to work hard and stay focused on my goal. I did not consider any other options and had no alternative plans in the event that I was not accepted into a medical school. Not getting into the medical school was not an option for me. I had a framed photo of Dr. Barnard on my desk. He became my source of encouragement. He gave me strength to push a little further each day. I kept saying to myself, "I will become a doctor, and someday, I will meet Dr. Barnard in person." During my first year in medical school, I did have the privilege of meeting him. He had traveled to Mumbai from South Africa to lecture at our medical school!

Was this all just a coincidence or somehow engineered and orchestrated by my subconscious mind, driven by my conscious thinking? What led me to eventually achieve my dream of becoming a doctor? What are the chances of this happening to a kid who grew up in a small village in Kenya?

During my last year in medical school, I set my goals on learning neurology in the United States and settling in that country. I was able to achieve both. I believe that, as soon as you conceive of an idea or a goal you want to accomplish, your subconscious mind finds a way to make it happen. How exactly it does thus, we do not yet know.

Perhaps the brain is supercharged and (consciously or subconsciously) picks up any valuable information it comes across and uses that information to push us in the right direction until the desired goal is achieved. Research supports the notion that even a small amount of positive thinking regularly strengthens your willpower (or perhaps your subconscious mind) to realize your goals. Regular meditation has been shown to sharpen that area of the brain that is responsible for positive thoughts.

According to Dr. Richard Davidson, a prominent neuroscientist at the University of Wisconsin–Madison who employs objective modern research tools, such as functional magnetic resonance imaging [fMRI], positron emission tomography [PET] scanners, and electroencephalogram [EEG] recordings: "The brain is an organ designed to change in response to experience. Through thought training, you can use the power of your mind to change the pathways in your brain."

Until science figures out how the subconscious mind and the conscious brain communicate with each other, what is the harm in commanding the subconscious mind to work for you to achieve the goals you so desire? My own experiences add further to my growing acceptance of the tremendous and the unexplained power of the subconscious mind.

* * * * *

I love to travel. Traveling nurtures the mind and the soul. It broadens our horizons and makes us more tolerant and accepting of the diversity in our world. And going places has never been so easy. Each year, I usually pick a place or a country I would like to visit, write it down on a piece of paper, and then keep that paper in my wallet. This allows me to pull it out and look at it when I have some moments to spare. I even visualize myself traveling to that place. It works every time! You may call it planning or something else, but I have always managed to travel to the country I pick for the year.

While on my flight home from Austria during the summer of 2004, I pulled out my diary planner and started to plan my trip for the following year. I closed my eyes and thought about places I would love to visit. There were so many of them, I could not focus on any one particular place. After a while, when I opened my eyes, right there in front of me was a newspaper in the seat pocket with an advertisement inviting me to visit Turkey. That convinced me. I wrote down "Turkey, 2005" on a piece of paper and tucked it into my wallet. I filed away the other countries I was dreaming about somewhere else in my brain to be retrieved later.

My focus from now on would be Turkey. It is amazing how, once you focus your mind on a subject, you begin to notice it everywhere. My brain's threshold for noticing anything about Turkey became very low. Before, even when something about Turkey was right in front of me, I would not notice it, but now, I began to be aware of it with ease. A few months after I had made up my mind, a two-page article on places to visit in Turkey appeared in our local Sunday newspaper.

Very soon after this, a local doctor came to see me in the clinic for some neurological problems. As we talked, I learned that he was from Turkey! He became very excited when I told him of my impending trip. This was the first time I had openly declared my intention to visit Turkey. I had not yet made any concrete plans; but somehow, I knew that my subconscious mind was at work, setting the stage for the actual trip to occur. Concentrating on my goals has always worked for me.

Even though I was sure about visiting Turkey, for some reason I had not yet made any travel arrangements. One morning, two envelopes from overseas arrived in the mail. I was being invited to present my work related to MS at the world's largest annual international conference devoted to basic and clinical research in MS, which was to be held in Thessaloniki, Greece. I looked at the map and found that Turkey bordered Greece; Thessaloniki didn't look too far from Istanbul. It was working. My subconscious mind was definitely planning the trip for me.

I asked a travel agent to book my trip to Turkey and to get me in to Thessaloniki a day before my presentation at the convention. There was no direct flight from Istanbul to Thessaloniki, so I agreed to take a twelve-hour journey by bus. My traveling companion and I had the most wonderful time in Turkey and finally boarded the bus early in the morning to head for Thessaloniki. We must have ridden for four hours when the bus made a stop at the border to have our passports checked. That is when the problems began.

The bus broke down. It would not start. There was something wrong with the engine, which (the drivers assured us) would be simple to fix, but three hours later, they were still working on it. Everyone on the bus were now concerned and started to approach other buses and private vehicles to see if they could get rides, but without much success. Another two hours passed; by now, I had also begun to worry. My presentation was scheduled for the following morning. Somehow, I had to reach Thessaloniki. But how could I do that? We were at least one hundred miles away from the next big town.

The driver finally got the word from the home office that a bus was being dispatched from Greece to pick

Bus breakdown at the border of Turkey and Greece, September, 2005. The driver worked hard to get the bus going but without any success. He even took off his shirt off, somewhat dramatically, to impress us that he meant business when it came to fixing the bus.

up all the stranded passengers. Assuming the bus would reach us at the specified time, it would get us into Thessaloniki much after my presentation was due to take place. I began to panic. But then I said to myself, "Stay calm, be positive, and invoke the power of the subconscious mind."

I closed my eyes and imagined myself presenting at the conference, and immediately I felt a little sense of control over the situation that had appeared to be so hopeless a few minutes ago.

When I opened my eyes, I saw a Mercedes Benz car pulling up to the immigration checkpoint. Everyone rushed to see if they could get a ride, and I saw the driver shaking his head from side to side, refusing their requests. I meditated for just a few more seconds and then approached the car, fully convinced that I would get a ride. As he lowered his window, I said, "Could you please give me a ride to the nearest town so that I can rent a car? I need to be in Thessaloniki by early morning."

He looked at me for a moment and then said that he and the other passenger sitting in the front seat were heading to Thessaloniki as well. Was this a coincidence? I offered to pay them for the ride. He told me that he didn't need the money, but would be happy to give me a ride. Since they had no luggage, the trunk was empty. I gestured to my friend to come over; we

The two gentlemen who gave us a ride in their Mercedes-Benz and dropped us off at the doorstep of our hotel in Thesssaloniki, Greece. From left to right: the author, Athinakis Michales, who has MS, and his business partner, Vasiliou Vasilis.

loaded the car, and off we went. The rest of the journey took eight hours; the driver dropped us off at the doorstep of our hotel.

There is more to this story. The other passenger, who was the owner of the car and a prominent industrialist in Greece, asked me why I was visiting Thessaloniki. I told him about the research I do in MS and that I had to be there in the morning to present the results of my research at a very large convention, the subject of which was MS. He turned around to look at me, and I could see tears welling up in his eyes as he finally said, "I am diagnosed with MS!"

I was speechless. Was this all a coincidence or a result of the power of positive thinking and the subconscious mind? I cannot prove it one way or the other, but what if it was due to the latter? And if this phenomenon is real and exists, then we would miss out a lot in life if we didn't practice it. However, if it is not real, and if it doesn't exist, how much do we lose by practicing it anyway?

I told my new friends who had given me the ride that we should take a photo together because, when I would tell this story back home in the United States, no one would believe me without proof.

I continue to practice what I have learned over the years. There are many excellent books written on the subject, but the one that I have found very beneficial is *The Power of Your Subconscious Mind* by Joseph Murphy. I pick it up every few months to reenergize my thinking.

* * * * *

Recently, I was on a flight to Milwaukee and met a very learned man who was sitting next to me. Dr. Jay Krachmer, an award-winning educator and a researcher, had recently retired as chair of the Department of Ophthalmology at the University of Minnesota. He was visiting Milwaukee to deliver a keynote speech at an ophthalmologists' convention. I asked him what his topic was, and he answered, "Disruptions." I didn't understand, so he clarified.

"It is becoming increasingly difficult to practice medicine these days without being interrupted," he explained. "As physicians, we are being drawn in different directions. We wear so many hats, all at the same time. We need to deal with hospital administrators and insurance companies, to be aware of the litigious society we live in; and even though we are never trained to be so, we must also be business savvy. And we are forced to do all this as we struggle to uphold our medical code of ethics."

He continued, "An additional, new disruption is mandatory electronic record keeping. We now have to assume the role of a clerk as well. Increasingly, a computer is becoming the interface between the doctor and the patient. If we do not act now, we will forget to be in the 'zone,' which is so vital and necessary in caring for our patients." He made a lot of sense to me. I could absolutely relate to what he was saying.

He said he always tried to get into the "zone" before he did any surgery or saw a patient in consultation.

"Sometimes, when I forget to do that," he continued, "I can tell the difference in my performance. When I get into the zone, the energy is different. It is much more positive, and I feel calm. I perform so much better. What is important is that when I am not in the zone, my patients can perceive the difference as well."

That ophthalmologist, who has taught hundreds of doctors in this area of specialization, has published more than one hundred original research papers in peer-reviewed scientific journals, and has written thirteen scientific books, knows what he is talking about. "To be in the zone, you have to clear your mind of all clutter and simply focus on your patient. You may say a short prayer if it helps, but most importantly, have a positive attitude."

Isn't this what prominent modern-day neuroscientists, such as Eccles and Davidson, have taught us based on their impressive scientific research? Positive thinking, the right mindset, and your subconscious mind power can lead to greater success, peace, and happiness. Invoking the power within you to reach your goal is really not a recently learned phenomenon. Matthew knew about it two thousand years ago.

Ask and it will be given to you; seek and you will find;
knock and the door will be opened to you.
For every one who asks receives; he who seeks finds;
and to him who knocks, the door will be opened.
—Matthew 7:7 (KJV)

11. DESTINY

I have no regrets in my life. I think that everything happens to you for a reason. The hard times that you go through build character, making you a much stronger person.
—Rita Mero

Learn to get in touch with the silence within yourself, and know that everything in life has purpose.
There are no mistakes, no coincidences.
All events are blessings given to us to learn from.
—Elisabeth Kübler-Ross, psychiatrist who wrote the groundbreaking book, *On Death and Dying*

"I do not care to live any more. I wish I were dead." Candice had reached the lowest point in her life and was inconsolable. Her marriage of twenty years had come to an end. Bruce, her husband, had dropped the bomb on her two days before her visit to see me in the clinic. He was having an affair with their neighbor and had moved in with her. It shocked me as well.

Bruce had been with her when she was diagnosed with MS some ten years ago. It was two days after she had delivered the last of their three children. I was called to examine her because of persistent numbness and weakness in her legs following an epidural she had received to ease the pain during birth of her daughter. When I saw her, she was also complaining of double vision. An MRI of her brain and spinal cord confirmed my clinical suspicion of MS.

It was a difficult conversation. How could I tell this young mother of three that she had been diagnosed with a disease that is the commonest cause of disability in young adults in this country—a disease that is permanent and has no cure? Knowing that a positive attitude does make a difference in a patient's medical outcome, I told her that MS today is not what it was ten years ago. We have learned a lot about the disease and developed effective therapies that prevent its progression. I had long-term studies to back up my statement.

She was not listening to me. The word MS had her thinking about her aunt, who had suffered from the disease and had been bedridden for several years before she died.

"Who will take care of my children? I want to raise them and see them grow," said Candice with tears running down her cheeks.

Bruce held her hand and tried to be supportive, but he was also visibly shaken by the diagnosis. Finally, he turned to Candice and said, "We will fight this together. We will get whatever help is needed. It will work out well. I love you, and I will be with you, always."

And Candice did well. Her follow-up visits to the clinic were down to every six months. She never returned to her nursing job after she was diagnosed with MS. Spending time with her children and husband was now more important to her. She walked with a cane, and even though she had more bad days than good, she took great pride in raising her three children. She took daily injections to prevent the progression of MS.

"A total of over three thousand injections," she had declared during her previous visit to the clinic. Her husband had been her rock all these years. If MS confined her to a wheelchair, she would still continue to move her life forward, knowing that her husband was by her side.

But now he was gone, and she had no strength left in her to get on with her life. She wanted to die. I tried to be reassuring and encourage her to continue trying, but I knew it was not working. I felt helpless, but then I remembered the true story I had just finished writing. I printed out a copy for her and said, "Candice, read this story. It will help you to understand why I believe that everything in life happens for a reason. Time not only heals the wound; it also opens doors to opportunities." Here is the story I shared with Candice.

* * * * *

"I am sending Illa to Milwaukee to live with you. Please take care of her," my father said to me during a long-distance phone call from India. He was asking me to undertake an enormous responsibility, a decision I am sure didn't come easily to him.

Many thoughts came to my mind as I hung up the phone. I remembered the night Illa was born in our two-story house in Machakos, Kenya. After a lot of shouts and cries and what seemed like an endless commotion in the adjoining bedroom, I heard her first cry! The youngest of my six sisters had arrived. I was ten years old then.

Now, twenty-six years later, she was about to begin her life in a new country, which I had adopted as my own. I never asked her, but I am sure it must have been a very emotional and a heart-wrenching decision for her as well.

My father was six years old when he and his mother left India to join his father in Kenya. He grew up, worked hard, and prospered. A few years after Kenya received its independence from the British in 1963, my parents decided to retire in India. With Illa, they settled in Rajkot, a fairly large city in the state of Gujarat, where Mahatma Gandhi had received his high school education more than one hundred years before.

Life was good for them. Illa did well in college and took art classes; in the years that followed, art would prove to be her calling. At that time, Illa was the person everyone in our family turned to when they visited India, especially when it came to shopping. Besides "coming home to parents," shopping for clothes and jewelry was always a high priority on their list of things to do.

Several memorable family weddings took place in Rajkot, thanks to Illa's superb organizational skills. My parents increasingly came to rely on her, and she sincerely enjoyed what she was doing. My parents' fiftieth wedding anniversary was coming up, and Illa declared to all of us, "This celebration would be the grandest of all the functions I have organized!"

The rest of her nine siblings, who all lived overseas, would arrive with our families just a few days before the party, so it was up to her to arrange everything. For the venue, she reserved the best banquet hall in the city and sent elaborate invitations to more than five hundred friends and extended family members in India and overseas.

She engaged several of the best chefs to prepare the food. The family home was decorated two weeks in advance with a fresh coat of paint, strings of lights were wrapped around the entire house, and beautifully embroidered ethnic door hangings called torans adorned the building. Well-known musicians and singers were invited to entertain the guests.

Illa had thought of everything, including six hundred mementoes, which she had wrapped herself in beautiful gold paper, for those who would come to one of the most enjoyable and elegant parties the city had seen in a long time.

Our siblings and their families were *en route* to Rajkot from Kenya, England, and the United States, when the tragedy occurred. My mother suffered a major heart attack and passed away within a few minutes. In accordance with the Hindu practice, she was taken to the cremation grounds within three hours after the doctor had declared her dead.

Illa was devastated. Months went by, but she didn't recover from the tragic event. Now concerned about her well-being, my father decided that Illa should come to America to live with me. He hoped a new environment would help heal the wound.

Illa did heal, but that process took a long time. She gradually began to paint and cook again. Then, after a while, she basically took over the kitchen. My younger brother, Yogesh, a university student, was living with us at the time. He invited some of his friends over for dinner, and soon the praise of Illa's cooking was the talk amongst all of his friends.

Yogesh was on the committee of the International Students Organization, and he was very popular with the Indian students. Being far away from home, they craved home-cooked Indian food, and Illa was a godsend to them. We had frequent dinner parties at our place. It became a routine to celebrate anyone's birthday with Illa's cooking and a homemade cake, followed by music and singing.

By this time, we had come to know a lot of students, so there was a party at least twice a month. Illa began to volunteer at the Art Museum and started to teach art to young children. It was good to see that she was healing, but she was also getting to an age when we needed to begin thinking about her

My father in the center with his children and grandchildren, ten days after the death of my mother. Being with family helped ease the pain of loss (Rajkot, India, 1984).

My siblings—six sisters (two from the UK, two from Kenya, and two who lived in India); three brothers (two from Kenya and one from the United States)—and my father and his younger sister, seated on the ground, ten days after the death of my mother. Illa is on the extreme right (Rajkot, India, 1984)

marriage. This weighed heavily on my heart as time went by. It was my father's desire to find a match that Illa would agree to, but it had to be within our caste. This is a formidable task in a country where our community is quite small and scattered. In addition, marriage was the furthest thing from Illa's mind.

My family belongs to the Kshatriya caste. It is ranked second among the four-caste system based on ancient Hindu scriptures called the *vedas*. The word "Kshatriya" means "power" and "ruler" and people of this caste were the protectors or rulers of communities and states in pre-independent India (prior to August 15, 1947).

In the ancient times, the caste system allowed for designation of special jobs such as Brahmins (the highest ranking) for religious functions, Vaishya (third ranking) responsible for business, and the Shudras (the lowest ranking) responsible for doing menial and unskilled jobs. Even though some form of caste system still exists in India, it is now considered it to be discriminatory.

Within each caste, there are further subdivisions called "communities," such as Patels, Shahs, and so on. I belong to the Gujarati Khatri community, with Gujarat being a state in India from which the current Prime Minister of India, Narendra Modi, hails. Within the communities are further subdivisions called "surnames." My surname is Katbamna. Marrying within the same last name is not allowed in the Hindu religion, unlike the Muslim religion, where marrying first cousins is not only allowed, but encouraged by families.

My father was against the caste system in that he firmly believed that all men are equal. The only reason he wanted Illa to marry a man from within the community was for "social reasons." In India, most the marriages are organized by parents, who play an active role in finding an appropriate match for their sons and daughters. So marrying within "the community" has advantages as well. You know the family you are getting married into, speak the same language, share the same dietary habits, and above all, it is much easier and quicker to forge a relationship between the two families because of the commonalities.

In Hindu tradition, every member of the immediate and extended family plays a significant and an important role in the wedding, which usually lasts for three days or more. The family relationship starts out with ease. Of course, marrying outside the community often works out as well, but it takes a lot of time and effort to develop the so-important family ties.

When I discussed this with Illa, I realized that she had not fully recovered from the loss of our mother that we had all suffered some two years before. Yet, I continued to search for a suitable match for her, hoping that when the time came, some of my sisters would talk to her and convince her to get married. It would be the right thing for her to do, we all agreed.

Soon, it became routine for me spend weekend mornings making phone calls to members of our community to inquire about whether they knew anyone else I could call. I became acquainted with practically all of the families of our caste who lived in the United States and Canada. A few prospective men did visit us, but Illa rejected them outright.

* * * * *

Eight thousand miles away, an Indian family from Tanzania had repatriated to India and settled in Rajkot, where my father lived. Mr. Shankarlal Joshi, a learned man, had been a principal and a teacher at a school in Tanzania for many years until he decided to retire with his wife and four children in India. Under his gentle guiding force, all of his children excelled in school and college.

One of his sons, Bharat, had placed first in his class on the electrical engineering school final examinations and received a letter from a university inviting him to earn his Ph.D. in Milwaukee, Wisconsin, in the United States. This excited Bharat. It was a great opportunity to advance his education in America, but "Where exactly is Milwaukee, and how do you properly pronounce the name?" he asked.

"It is far away. It is a different world, and we do not know any one close to us out there. Besides, there are excellent colleges in India where you can work on your Ph.D.," urged his father.

But Bharat was already dreaming of being in America and the future it held for him. He was determined. He started asking his friends if they knew of anyone in Milwaukee—someone he could call if he needed help. It would then make it easier to convince his parents. He called on his professor to discuss his plans to pursue further education overseas.

"Milwaukee! My neighbor's son lives there," said the professor.

"Destiny is at work!" was the immediate thought that came to Bharat.

"Come to my home in the evening," the professor suggested. "I will take you to my neighbor's house. I am sure he will help."

Bharat's heart was racing as he entered the house and took a seat in front of my father. "Will he help?" he wondered. Bharat studied my father's face for any expressions that would indicate his level of interest, as the professor narrated the reason of their visit.

"I am proud of your achievement, and I am excited that you will be going to where my son lives," said my father. Half way through writing the letter of recommendation addressed to me, however, he looked up at Bharat and then suddenly tore up the letter. Bharat's heart sank! My father was his only chance, and now he had backed off!

"I will not write this letter," said my father. "When you get to Milwaukee, call my son. I am confident he will welcome you and give you all the help you need. If he doesn't do that, then, I want you to give me a call!"

A letter would have been just great, thought Bharat. At least it would reassure his parents. He looked at the professor, hoping that he could convince the older man to write the letter, but the professor simply smiled at him and said, "Trust him."

* * * * *

We were in the midst of celebrating Yogesh's birthday when Bharat called to introduce himself. He had been in Milwaukee for a week and was already feeling homesick.

"We are having a party at my place. Get ready, and I will pick you up in fifteen minutes," I said.

His department at the university had found him an accommodation at a nearby rooming house that was very popular with the Indian students. He had a wonderful time that evening, and since he was a strict vegetarian, as we were, he ate very well that day. Bharat, like some of the other students, soon became a "regular" at our home. We enjoyed his company. Not only did he speak our language, but he had also grown up in East Africa as we had. Sometimes, we would converse in Swahili, the official language of the East African countries. He was also a teetotaler, giving us one more thing in common.

The year went by fast. Illa had finished her first major artwork in America. We framed it and hung it in the study, just in time to celebrate her birthday. With little help from the rest of us, Illa had prepared the food for some one hundred people. We were having a good time, and as I went into the study to answer the phone, I saw Bharat standing before the artwork. He seemed to be totally immersed in it.

I watched him for a few moments and then went up to him and asked, "What do you think about this piece of art?"

"It is simply breathtaking! A lot of love and soul has been poured into this painting."

He turned to me and asked, "Where did you get this painting? Who is the artist?"

It was then that I had an epiphany: Bharat would be a perfect match for Illa! He had been right there before my eyes these past two years; yet this thought had never crossed my mind. He was from a different caste than the one our family belonged to. According to Indian tradition, my father wanted Illa to be married within our caste. The question was would he agree to this proposal? And even if he did, would Illa and Bharat agree? I confided in Yogesh and was relieved to hear that he thought it was a great idea.

Quietly, we began to strategize about how to get Illa and Bharat to get to know each other better without revealing our intentions. On party days, we would ask Bharat if he could come early to help out in the kitchen. Once he arrived, all of us would conveniently disappear, leaving Illa and Bharat alone at home.

It worked! Soon they felt very comfortable with each other. They talked and laughed, and he stayed behind to talk with Illa, even after the other guests had left. Gradually, his visits to our home increased in frequency. After dinner, he and Illa would go for long walks.

Finally, one evening, I asked *the question*—"Would you consider getting married to each other?" To my delight, they both said "yes!"

Bharat and Illa with my father in the center after their engagement (Milwaukee, Wisconsin, 1987).

Wedding registration ceremony at my home with Illa (center),
my father and myself (Milwaukee, Wisconsin, 1988).

Bharat (in a white suit) on his wedding day with his father to his right,
his best-man to his left, and my father (Machakos, Kenya, 1988).

I called my father and explained that Bharat and Illa liked each other and wanted to get married but not without the blessings of their parents. My father wanted to know more about Bharat. As I explained that his family was from Tanzania, but now settled in Rajkot, he immediately recalled the meeting he had with the young man two years ago!

"If he is the same boy," he said, "they have my blessings. I remember that his professor, who is our neighbor, spoke very highly of him."

Bharat had never mentioned to me that he had met my father.

The wedding ceremony took place in Machakos, Kenya, in the same two-story house in which we had been raised. The reception was held in a very large community hall to accommodate more than four hundred guests. As soon as everyone was seated, my father stood up to make a speech.

He was visibly choked up with emotion, as he turned to Bharat's parents and said, "Two years ago, your son came to me—a stranger, wanting me to write a letter of recommendation to my son in Milwaukee. I refused to do that because I had confidence in the upbringing of my children that they would give help even to strangers, if help was needed. I did not have the slightest idea that it was my future son-in-law who was sitting before me that day. And now, I am giving my daughter away to him in marriage!"

Bharat and Illa have now been married for twenty-six years. Illa is a successful artist, and Bharat is a professor at a prestigious university in the United States. They have a son in medical school who is determined to be a neurologist.

* * * * *

Gradually, over the years that followed, Candice was able to change her outlook. She started to live again, but this was not an overnight conversion. Many events took place along the way that helped her to see her life as rewarding and worth living.

She became closer to her children. Her daughter finished college and got married. Candice even realized that she would not be the person she had become if her husband had stayed by her side. Over time, she had adopted the philosophy that everything in life happens for a reason.

Candice came to my office for her regular annual clinic visit, six years after her divorce. Her face beaming with happiness, she placed her two-month-old grandson in my arms. She couldn't have been any happier.

As I reflect on all the changes that have taken place in Candace's life, as well as my own, I ask myself: Is it destiny that orchestrates our lives, or are many of the events that take place driven by our desires and beliefs? How can I explain the way in which the sudden death of my mother, just a few days before her fiftieth wedding anniversary, proved to be the happiest way to memorialize a sad moment? All her children and family and friends were together to celebrate her life during the most tragic day in our lives.

How can I explain the most heartbreaking pain her death caused Illa? Yet had our mother not died, would Illa have come to America to find a new life and her husband? I choke up even now, when I think about young Bharat going to my dad, hoping to get a letter, being refused, but receiving much more than he could have ever asked for in the years to come.

Are these occurrences simply coincidences, or were they craftily orchestrated by destiny? While it is, of course, impossible to prove either of these alternatives, in my opinion, it is the latter. As I look back over my own life and the lives of many of my patients—Candice in particular—I remain convinced that destiny plays a bigger role than we may yet realize.

12. EMOTIONAL CLOSURE

Deposits of unfinished grief reside in more American hearts than I ever imagined. Until these pockets are opened and their contents aired openly, they block unimagined amounts of human growth and potential. They can give rise to bizarre and unexplained behavior which causes untold internal stress.
—Robert Kavanagh

He wept, and it felt as if the tears were cleansing him, as if his body needed to empty itself.
—Lois Lowry

I t was time to celebrate. During the last few weeks, ever since Idi Amin, the president of Uganda, had ordered the expulsion of his country's Asian minorities, tension in the Indian community had been running high. This was their home, their country. Their grandparents and parents had immigrated from India to help build Uganda, then under the British rule.

Hard-working people, they had excelled, not only in business, but also in the education, health, tourism, and banking industries; they were considered to be the backbone of the Ugandan economy.

Amin declared one morning that he had a dream in which God told him to order the expulsion. It was now official. Asians were given ninety days to leave the country. The systematic and ruthless ethnic cleansing of the Indians in Uganda had begun. News was slowly trickling in from the north that the military was looting Indian shops and homes and raping Indian women at gunpoint.

The head of the most famous and powerful Indian business family, which contributed about ten percent to Uganda's gross national product and employed more than 10,000 people, was imprisoned by Idi Amin, sending a ripple of fear through the Indian Community. If the so-called "Rockefeller of Uganda" could be brought to his knees in a rat-infested, dark cell in a filthy jail, there was no hope for ordinary Asians.

That was Sunday, November 5, 1972, which also happened to be *Diwali*—the "Festival of Lights"—the most important one-day festival in Hinduism, the religion practiced by a majority of the Ugandan Indians. All of the ten Indian families living just a few miles east of Jinja, the second largest town in Uganda, had gathered that day at the home of Dr. Desai to celebrate what would be their last Diwali in the country they had called their home. They wanted it to be a memorable one, about which they could tell stories to their grandchildren in the years to come, in some foreign country that would grant them refugee status. The women had put on their finest saris with bright, vibrant colors. They wore their gold necklaces, bangles, and diamonds on one side of their noses.

Rumor had it that when the government issued each of the families a date by which they must leave the country, they were not allowed to take anything of value with them. Amin wanted all the wealth belonging to the Indians to be distributed to the natives. The economy would be put in the hands of "black Ugandans" he had said.

This was the families' last chance to enjoy what they had. They had prepared an enormous variety of food to feast on and had delegated to the native Ugandan servants the task of arranging a buffet-style dinner. The children were happily lighting firecrackers in the huge enclosed compound of Dr. Desai's home. The men were sitting in a circle reminiscing about the good times they had had in Jinja, about Amin's madness, and the uncertainty of where their destinies would take them next. They had all grown up together, but this would be the last time they would celebrate Diwali with old friends or perhaps even see one another.

Dr. Desai was busy making *rangoli* just inside the entranceway to the compound that led to his home. Rangoli is artwork painted with a beautiful combination of colors on the floor at the doorstep of one's house to welcome Lakshmi, the goddess of wealth, as well as guests, into one's home. Rangoli patterns grace the entrance of every Hindu home during Diwali.

Dr. Desai was well known for his rangoli skills. People would drive up from Kampala, the largest Ugandan city, to admire his handiwork, which he created with a wide assortment of colored chalks and powders. This year, he wanted to make his rangoli special, so he decided to do it with oil paint that would last for years to come. He couldn't fight back the tears as he gave it his last finishing touch and signed his name.

Everyone agreed that the food was the best they had enjoyed in a long time. Finally, it was time to have some fun. At the urging of Mrs. Desai, a few of the guests agreed to sing some nostalgic Hindi film songs; soon, the rest of them joined in as well. A harmonium and Indian drums called tablas were produced for two teenaged boys, who had learned to play them at the Sunday temple school.

The music and singing continued well into the night, with a cool breeze from the east bringing in the sweet scents emitted from the local sugar factory, one owned by an Indian family, and one of the largest in the world. No one wanted the celebration or the night to end. The morning would bring back the harsh reality of the expulsion.

Suddenly, there was a loud explosion just outside the house, followed by the rapid firing of rifle shots. The music stopped abruptly. Just as a few of the men ran toward the compound door to see what was happening outside, the door was thrown open, and Amin's soldiers marched right into the compound. Their leader quickly lined the men up against the compound wall. The women were ordered into a room, and the children, who were now trembling with fear, huddled in the kitchen.

The soldiers pointed rifles at their heads and ordered the women to remove all the gold they were wearing. As one of the women struggled to get the tight-fitting bangles off her wrist, a sharp blow to her head with a rifle butt caused her to collapse on the floor, unconscious. One of the younger women rushed to her aid, but a soldier grabbed her by her hair, threw her to the floor, and started to forcibly undress her. She pleaded for him not to hurt her, but he continued to tear into her clothes, like a pit bull attacking a helpless victim with unstoppable aggression.

"Kill me first!" shouted her husband, as he ran to her rescue. The soldier looked up at him and their eyes locked.

"*Daktari! Doctor!*" the soldier said in a surprised voice. Six years earlier, this doctor had saved the life of the soldier, who moments before had been about to molest the doctor's wife.

The soldier, then a sixteen-year-old boy, had been brought to a rural hospital at 1 o'clock in the morning, burning with high fever, delirious, and with a distended abdomen. The doctor very quickly realized that the young man had a burst appendix with a localized intra-abdominal abscess. He would surely die without emergency surgery. He needed to be taken to a bigger hospital in Kampala, but he could not possibly survive the arduous, four-hour-long journey.

The boy's parents pleaded with the doctor to do whatever he could do to save their son. The rural hospital was not set up to give general anesthesia, which was required for a major surgery such as this. Could he possibly get by using a local anesthetic? There was no time to think.

The boy took a turn for the worse. With his blood pressure dropping, he lapsed into a coma. The doctor made the bold decision to operate on him. He sent the ward boy to quickly fetch back-up nurses and when he finally made an incision on the boy's abdomen, the electricity went off. It was pitch dark until the ward boy lit some candles. The generator had been out of service for some months; the government had yet to send someone to repair it.

The doctor performed the surgery in three hours under a kerosene lantern held above the field of surgery. It was a long recovery process, but under the doctor's excellent care, the boy was able to walk away from the hospital six weeks later. The doctor did not charge for his medical services, but even if he had, the boy's parents would have had nothing with which to pay him.

As that young man—now a soldier—stood up, he didn't say anything further to the doctor, but he ordered the rest of the soldiers to leave these Indians alone. With the loot in their backpacks, they left the compound as quickly as they had stormed in.

All of the Indians, now consumed with fear, huddled together. No one spoke. The children were too scared to even cry. Finally, the doctor said softly how God has plans for everything. Had he not treated this young man and saved his life, he and his wife and countless others might have been killed or at least suffered brutally at the hands of the young soldiers.

He asked with a slightly louder voice as he shook his head from side to side, "What will happen when all the Indian doctors leave the country in ninety days, as ordered by Idi Amin? Indian doctors care for the majority of Ugandans, including Idi Amin. You know Dr. C. G. Patel? He is Idi Amin's personal physician. He, too, has been asked to leave."

Three days later, the Desai family received orders to leave the country within twenty-four hours. The fifty-mile drive from their home to the Entebee International Airport was the most fear-filled journey they had ever taken. They were stopped by makeshift military blockades five times. Each time, they were asked to step out of their car and were thoroughly searched, with guns pointed at their heads to make sure they didn't have any valuables on them. A wristwatch, given to Dr. Desai at his high school graduation by his grandfather, was snatched away from him at one of the checkpoints.

They finally made it to the airport, parked, left the car keys in the ignition, said goodbye to their car, and walked away. Their only possessions were the clothes they were wearing. Four hours later, they were airborne, scheduled to reach London in ten hours. Dr. Desai wept like a child as he looked down on the land they were leaving behind but, at the same time, was deeply relieved to have escaped from the brutal and unpredictable regime of Idi Amin.

From the time he had seized power in a military coup in 1971 to his flight from the country to a safe haven in Saudi Arabia seven years later, Amin had become to be known as the "Butcher of Uganda." History would record him as the most notorious of all of Africa's post-independence dictators. It is estimated that the number of his opponents who were either killed or tortured exceeded half a million people. Most of them were thrown into the Nile River, there to be eaten by crocodiles.

On his flight to London, Dr. Desai knew that even though he had to leave all his possessions and valuables behind, his soul had not been robbed by Amin. As he wept, his resolve to build a life for his family of five in a foreign country became even stronger. He remembered his grandfather, who had arrived penniless in Jinja from a faraway country; he had prospered and shared his good fortune with the locals by building an elementary school and a small hospital.

When his grandfather had first arrived, there had been no electricity or running water in the village. He had to build a shelter for himself using corrugated iron sheets. But he was a resilient young man. He didn't know how to read or write, but he was a hard worker with good, enterprising ideas that he transformed into reality over the years. He became a very prosperous businessman and made a fortune, which he wisely shared with the local community. Dr. Desai had his grandfather's genes! He resolved to work hard and succeed in the country that granted him and his family asylum.

'God' tells Amin to expel Asians, the majority of whom were Indians, as dreams quickly turn to nightmares. Expelled Indians in Uganda find refuge in the UK.

Ugandan Asians arrive in the UK after being expelled by Idi Amin in 1972. More than 60,000 Asians were expelled.

One of the refugee camps that housed the displaced Indians who arrived in the UK. The few remaining buildings left at the camp today.
(Credit: ITV News)

The majority of the seventy thousand Asians who were expelled from Uganda settled in England without much more than the clothes they had on their backs. They worked hard and prospered. Forty-two years after their deportation, many are now multi-millionaires and recognized by Prime Minister David Cameron for their "extraordinary contribution to the national economy and to the fabric of British life."

* * * * *

The first two decades after the Asians first landed in the UK were very tough. The cold, damp weather, coupled with mental anguish caused by discrimination against the refugees, was difficult to overcome for many. Most of the refugees readily found work in factories, some working double shifts. Women who had never worked outside their homes in Uganda were now forced to take up jobs to provide for their families.

The Dave (pronounced Dah-Veh) family of four was one of many such families. Their forty years in London went by quickly in some ways and slowly in others. Yogesh, the eldest of the Dave boys, and was thirteen when he left Uganda, was now a young man working as an automotive mechanic. He quoted Charles Dickens in describing the thirty-year period: "It was the best of times, and it was the worst of times."

Yogesh married a beautiful Indian girl from Kenya. Their upcoming vacation to Kenya stirred some longings in him to return to Uganda to visit his birthplace. He had been so busy making a life for himself in the UK that he had little time to dwell on his memories of growing up in Uganda. He never imagined that he would one day be able to visit his birthplace. He now felt drawn to visit Lugazi, since it was only a ninety-minute flight from Nairobi, the capitol city of Kenya, where he would be vacationing.

As he stepped out of the car on the main street of Lugazi, he was anxious and apprehensive about not knowing how he was going to react to a place he had once called his home, one that he had been forced to leave some four decades before. His heart raced. Nothing he saw looked familiar to him.

The street was lined with shops on either side with open sewage flowing in the roadside gutters. The area was littered with garbage. It was crowded with hundreds of people, some standing idle and others busy shopping. There were coffee and tea stalls every one hundred feet or so on the main street and each one of them was playing loud local music on their transistor radios. These stalls seemed to be popular and attracted crowds, some watchers sitting on a wooden bench and others squatting on the ground as they sipped their brew or simply listened to the music.

Even though he was physically present, Yogesh did not feel at all connected to the town. He wanted to see the house in which he had spent the first years of his life. Would it still be there, and if so, in what condition? If people lived there now, who were they?

Yogesh's childhood home in Uganda.

Forty-year-old rangoli on the door-step of Yogesh's childhood home, painted by his father.

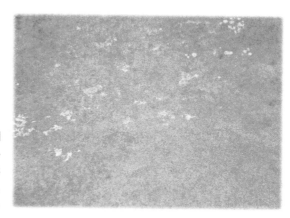

Would they let him in? His heart beat faster as he quickened his pace in the direction he believed his former home to be.

Suddenly, he was standing in front of the building he had once called home. It looked exactly as he remembered it. Nothing much had changed, yet he felt like a stranger.

Forty years in England was a long time. From the time he had arrived as a teenager to becoming a successful auto mechanic, Yogesh's life had taken many turns, both good and bad. He had traveled so much and so far in his life, but for the house before him, it seemed that time had stood still. His experience thus far felt completely surreal. He spoke in broken and rusty Swahili to the current occupants and explained who he was.

As Yogesh took the first step inside the compound, his right foot landed on the faded rangoli painted so many years ago by his father. When he looked at the colored pattern on the floor, an avalanche of emotions hit him and he started to sob uncontrollably. It all came back to him. His father had painted the rangoli with oil paints during the last Diwali they had celebrated in their home.

This house, which had seemed so distant and strange only moments before, now felt close to him. Yogesh, who had seen his parents and other expatriate families work hard all their lives, making countless sacrifices to raise their children and provide them with a proper education, recalled his own struggles growing up in a different country, where racial slurs were so common he barely noticed them after a while.

All of his suppressed emotions erupted as he placed his foot on the faded rangoli that day, producing a catharsis that brought healing to so many wounds he had carried with him throughout the years. In that moment, Yogesh felt as though a huge weight had been lifted from his beck. He felt lighter. He could breathe. He had achieved emotional closure.

Yogesh Dave is my brother-in-law.

* * * * *

Letting go of the past is very important for healing the soul. The ending of an important part of your life may be difficult and even painful. Memories held within your subconscious mind—good or bad— can profoundly affect your physical and mental health. The majority of the Ugandan Asians put the past behind them and forged ahead with resolve, determination, and resilience to succeed in a foreign country. As they aged, their emotional wounds healed, but not permanently. When placed in a situation that reminded them of the loss, emotions would surface. Memories are never lost. They are imbedded in the brain.

Closure is extremely important after any emotional trauma. If you don't find peace within yourself, the suppressed emotional memories can affect you psychologically, retard your personal growth, and even lead to physical ailments. Understanding how this mind-body connection works and applying new, effective tools for releasing emotions is often the key to rapid healing. Finding such closure, however, may not always be easy or forthcoming. Talking about your experience with others who have been through similar situations, reliving it in a controlled, simulated environment, or letting go of emotions with professional help is useful.

There are many good studies that link anger, hostility, and anxiety to coronary artery disease. In his groundbreaking book, *Reversing Heart Disease*, Dr. Dean Ornish demonstrates that even severe coronary heart disease can be reversed without drugs or surgery. He is the first clinician to offer documented proof that heart disease can be halted, or even reversed, simply by changing your lifestyle and letting go of your destructive emotions.

* * * * *

After fighting a losing war against Tanzania under President Julius Nyerere, Idi Amin was exiled from Uganda on April 11, 1979, and fled to Libya. He died of kidney failure on August 16, 2003, in Jeddah, Saudi Arabia. A plea by his family to have him buried in his birth country was denied by the present Ugandan government, which had begun to woo the once-expelled Indians back from Britain

In 1982, the government enacted the Expropriated Properties Bill, which provided for the restoration of property to Asians expelled under Amin. By 1983, about six thousand Asians had returned. The sugar factory, which was in total ruin, was rehabilitated by its original Indian owners. While it had once produced only fifty thousand tons of sugar, by 1985, its production more than tripled.

For some of the Asians, a short return trip to Uganda and to the homes they had been forced to abandon on such a short notice was what they needed to heal their souls. When they closed their eyes, they could see the evidence of their interrupted lives—a fridge filled with vegetables and milk, freshly washed clothes hanging on a sisal rope outside in the yard to dry, three generations of priceless memorabilia, the pets they could not take with them. These losses had caused deep emotional wounds. Coming home at last provided emotional closure.

13. CROSSING THE BOUNDARY

Love is our true destiny. We do not find the meaning of life by ourselves alone. We find it with another.
—Thomas Merton

All religions, arts and sciences are branches of the same tree. All these aspirations are directed toward ennobling man's life, lifting it from the sphere of mere physical existence and leading the individual towards freedom.
—Albert Einstein, *Moral Decay*, first published in 1937

B y the time he finished taking care of his last patient in the morning, Dr. Ahmad was exhausted. He had woken up with a mild headache, but didn't think much about it. He blamed it on the calls he had from the hospital that had interrupted his sleep several times during the night. Now, as he sat down in the recliner for a cup of coffee, he started to perspire and realized that his vision was not right. He couldn't read numbers on the clock that hung on his office wall. He closed his eyes and tried to relax before the afternoon clinic, which would begin in an hour. A little rest and a quiet time would surely energize him, he thought.

The nurse found him fast asleep when she went to inform him of the next patient who was waiting to see him. She touched him to wake him up, but was alarmed to note that his body was burning with fever and drenched in sweat. Before she could decide what to do next, his body began to shake uncontrollably, his eyes rolled up, and his teeth bit hard on his protruding tongue, causing blood-tinged, frothy secretions to ooze from his mouth. The nurse yelled for help and called 911.

A spinal tap confirmed that Dr. Ahmad was suffering from encephalitis, a viral infection of the brain. Although the confirmatory test would take two days, the doctors were quite sure of their diagnosis: herpes encephalitis, the most common form of potentially fatal encephalitis in the United States, with a mortality rate of 15 percent at three months!

Even with the most effective antiviral drug therapy available, fewer than 40 percent of patients survive with minimal or no long-term neurologic complications. Within twelve hours of waking up that morning with a headache, Dr. Ahmad was now comatose and had to be placed on a respirator.

"The next few days are very critical," the neurologist told Mrs. Ahmad, who felt as though a tornado had hit her. All she could do was slowly nod her head and thank the doctor for all his help. Until yesterday, her husband had been a vibrant, energetic, young man. Now, he looked so helpless with multiple tubes running in and out of his body. Yet, he also looked very peaceful, and except for his chest bellowing in and out with each respirator-driven breath, he lay there motionless. At least, he did not appear to be in pain.

After a thorough neurological examination, the doctor threw the stethoscope around his neck and looked at Mrs. Ahmad, who was sitting at her husband's bedside. She had not left his side in the last five days. Working as a full-time financial planner, she normally spent several hours a day on the Internet checking the stock market to stay informed about what was happening in the rest of the world. Now, none of that mattered to her. It was as though she had been transported to a different world, a world she had not known before.

She peered at the doctor's face, seeking clues that would indicate any good news for her. Her husband's condition had not improved in the last five days, and she could now sense that the doctors were becoming less optimistic.

"No major changes," declared the neurologist. "But at least he is not worse, and that is good." It is amazing how the loved ones of critically ill not only grasp at every word that is spoken to them, but can also sense what the doctors are not saying. Their body language and tone of voice reveal much more than their words. Mrs. Ahmad searched the doctor's face, and for the first time, he did not meet her eyes. Her heart sank. She knew the doctors were doing the best they could. They were his friends and colleagues in the hospital. But her husband was not getting better.

What else could she do? The longer he remained in a coma, the worse the outcome, according to the infectious disease specialist. All she could do was to pray and remain at his bedside. She was aware of the power of prayer. Positive outcomes have been associated with prayers in various clinical trials, but she also knew that unless the prayers were offered with a deep conviction and an unwavering faith in God, they might not have a significant healing effect. On the other hand, the powerful energy produced by a focused meditative mind had been proven to have a positive influence on people around you. So she prayed and channeled all her positive conscious thoughts towards her husband.

"He is perhaps a shade worse today," his neurologist said with a serious look on his face. "It is the eighth day today. We are doing all we can, but he doesn't seem to be responding as we had hoped. We will continue to treat him aggressively, and let us hope and pray for him to turn around."

The doctor's words hit Mrs. Ahmad like a brick, shattering the glimmer of hope she had been clinging to. She felt drained of energy as a cold shiver ran through her body. The doctor was talking to her, but she could not hear him. He seemed so far away. She felt numb.

As she turned to look at her husband, tears poured down her cheeks. She closed her eyes and sat at his bedside, holding his hand. To her, it felt as if she had been zoned out for a very long time, but only five minutes had elapsed when she opened her eyes again. She felt lighter and no longer had the dreadful sinking feeling she had been experiencing for the last few days. Her mind and body were renewed and energized, ready to take on the world. It was an incredible feeling of hope. She had experienced this once before, immediately after she had given birth to her son.

The following morning, she came early to pray by his bedside. Her cell phone rang. The area code indicated the call to be from Chicago. The Imam must be here, she thought. He had accepted her request to come and pray for her husband and had called three hours earlier to say that he was on his way.

"We are in the midst of a blizzard, and the heavy snow fall has reduced traffic to a snail's pace. It may be another six hours before I am able to reach the hospital," the Imam told her. Because of their intense and unconditional devotion to the Prophet Mohammad and Allah, Mrs. Ahmad wanted the Imam to touch her husband and pray for him.

It was Friday, an important day of the week in Islam. Friday carries many virtues and blessings and the power of prayers offered on this day is well recognized in Quran. Her mind, troubled by the fact that the Imam was not able to make it, began to race in different directions.

Just then, she saw Father Joe, a Catholic priest, walk into the intensive care unit carrying a Bible in his left hand, close to his chest. Mrs. Ahmad looked at the priest for a moment and without any hesitation, walked over to him and asked, "Father, will you please read Quran to my husband?"

For a moment, Father Joe froze. No one before had ever approached him to read Quran. He looked into Mrs. Ahmad's eyes and then at her husband. "Of course!" he replied

After reading from the Quran for two hours, Father Joe looked at Dr. Ahmad, placed his right hand over his forehead, and in a very calm, soothing voice, talked to him. "This is Father Joe. Open your eyes if you can hear me." Dr. Ahmad opened his eyes!

Dr. Ahmad made an excellent recovery and continues to run his thriving practice.

Wanting to learn what compelled a Muslim woman to approach a Catholic priest and for him to accept this most incredible request, I could not wait to interview both of them. Father Joe agreed to meet me for lunch at a quiet restaurant. Casablanca on Brady Street at 12:00 noon, I thought, would be good. Besides, the food served during the lunch hour is all vegetarian, which suited me well. However, I didn't know until I reached the restaurant that the entire street had been blocked off that day to celebrate Brady Street Days, with loud music, different ethnic foods, beer, and a lot of people.

Twenty minutes later, I spotted Father Joe walking toward the restaurant, sweating profusely on this hot summer day, and holding on to several books. He had parked his car a mile away.

"I am so sorry," I said. "Let us find another place to go to."

He smiled, declined my offer, and gestured for me to sit down at a table inside the restaurant, where the music was no less deafening than on the street. We spent the next three hours conversing, totally oblivious to what was going on around us.

The books he was carrying were for me to read later. For now, we discussed about Christianity and what his faith meant to him.

"Why are the Christians so intolerant of other faiths and beliefs?" I asked. To support this statement I read out to him from my prepared notes, what Jesus is believed to have said, "I am the way, and the truth, and the life; no one comes to the Father, but through Me." (John 14:6). I also reminded Father Joe that before becoming pope, Cardinal Ratzinger was known for his intolerant views about Islam. Within a year of being appointed the spiritual leader to more than a billion Roman Catholics, his remarks at a speech in

Germany were perceived to be derogatory towards Islam, inviting some harsh criticism from Islamic countries around the world. In fact, the only pope to have ever entered a mosque was Pope John Paul II in 2001.

"So, given this background, why did you, as a Catholic priest, agree to hold Quran and read from it to Dr. Ahmad?" I inquired, truly wishing to know.

Father paused for a while and answered, "To me, the few steps that Mrs. Ahmad took toward me that day were the giant steps for mankind," drawing an analogy to the first sentence Neil Armstrong uttered when he landed on the moon in 1969. "In those few seconds, she had crossed all of the man-made boundaries and entered into the higher field of spirituality. In this field, you communicate freely, without any restrictions or prejudice towards other human beings. What I saw in her eyes electrified me. It ignited in me the courage to rise to her plane. I had to meet her at her spiritual level. I would have been a failure in my own mind as a clergy if I didn't, and I would have regretted it for the rest of my life."

Father Joe had been inspired to cross the boundary. What if we break down all of the man-made religious boundaries? What if we tear down the walls that keep us away from each other and enter into one zone called "the spiritual world"? Would not this liberate us from what is at the heart of the present-day crisis and intolerance in this world?

Rigid, man-made rules to govern the faithful are choking us, robbing us of our ability to think, and destroying the very fiber of our moral being. Religions of the world that are designed to instill fear, rather than promote respect, love, and tolerance toward one another, have consumed more lives than any other cause in the history of mankind.

I asked Father Joe, "If you accept that the ultimate goal of any human being should be to rise beyond organized religion to a spiritual level, then why don't you give up being a Catholic priest and just be a "spiritual clergy? Not only have you been there, but you are there!"

He smiled again, placed his hand lightly on mine, and said, "If you uproot a tree, it dies! I have been

Fr. Joseph (Joe) Bisoffi was born in Trentino, Italy and joined the Order of St. Camillus in 1964. The primary mission of the order is the care of the sick. Father Joe came to the United Stated in 1969 to study theology in Boston, MA, and was ordained in Italy on June 24, 1972. He retired in 2008.

able to reach where I am because of the nourishment I received from the religion I have adopted as my own. Leaving it behind would be like cutting off my legs. And without my legs, I wouldn't be able to move around; I wouldn't be able to live. I would die just as the tree would without its roots."

His answer reminded me of Mahatma Gandhi, whose keen interest in Christianity and his appreciation of the selfless love offered by Jesus had often prompted the question about why he didn't convert to Christianity. He answered, "Even though I like my friend's mother very much, I do not have to give up mine!"

Religion should be a stepping stone to reach higher ground. Just as you go through life's milestones, so must you go through spiritual milestones. When you get stuck at one level and fail to grow, so does your spirituality. This stagnation can breed religious fanaticism. Religious fanatics are those who are only capable of visualizing black and white. When a bird's wings are clipped, its world becomes very small and limited. When people don't grow, their world becomes small and limited as well. This fosters hatred instead of love, and love is the oxygen of life. Gandhi summed this up so beautifully: "If love was not the law of life, life would not have persisted in the midst of death."

So what fosters love, tolerance, respect for life, and eventually reaching the level where Mrs. Ahmad and

Father Joe met? Could it be the moral values instilled by parents, religious leaders of the world, teachers in schools, or perhaps the sum total of all of these influences?

Many respected leaders, including Gandhi, maintain that religion is the bedrock of moral order. But it is also true that where religion is too strong, it can cause cruelty and breed fanaticism, which in turn leads to bloodshed in the name of God.

How can you reconcile these fundamentally opposing views? Is that why the founding fathers insisted on separation of church and state in governing this country? If religion laid the foundation for Father Joe to reach higher ground, why doesn't it work for others?

Father Joe gave us the answer when he referred to the tiny steps taken by Mrs. Ahmad as "the giant step for mankind." Mrs. Ahmad's reaching out to Father Joe exemplifies the importance of building bridges in order to communicate with other religions and cultures and foster love and respect for our fellow human beings.

A recent example of such an effort was the spectacular dedication of one of the most beautiful temples built in New Delhi, India. This temple, which was built by the Hindus, was inaugurated on November 6, 2005, by the President of India, Dr. A.P.J. Abdul Kalam (a Muslim) in the presence of the Prime Minister of India, Mr. Manmohan Singh (a Sikh), the Leader of Opposition in the Indian Parliament, Mr. L. K. Advani (a Hindu), and Defense Minister A K Antony (a Christian).

* * * * *

What had prompted Mrs. Ahmad to reach out to a Catholic priest? I couldn't wait to ask her. She readily agreed, and arrived promptly on time to meet with me at my office. She was wearing a *hijab*, the most visible manifestation of a Muslim woman's faith. Except for her face and hands, she was covered with light-colored, traditional *salwar-kameez* outfit.

I have not studied Islam and I have read only parts of Quran but during the hour I spent with Mrs. Ahmad, I began to understand what Father Joe was able to recognize so readily by looking into her eyes that day in the ICU.

Her strong conviction in her faith was so very evident in the first few minutes of our conversation. Yet, she was also respectful of other religions of the world. To her, it was very simple: intolerance of other religions or faiths is a disease. Like cancer, it grows. The only effective weapon left to fight back this malignant growth is controlled by the religious leaders of the world. Education is very important. They need to teach the importance of compassion, love, respect, and tolerance of one another. "Religion and hatred do not go together," she stated. "Religion itself does not kill. It is the fear and the need to be powerful that kill. So many of the religious leaders are consumed with power and trapped in the web of material world and, as a result, have lost their ability to guide."

Religion to Mrs. Ahmad was a way to become a good human being to your family, to your neighbors, and to other fellow beings on this earth. She attributes her spiritual growth to praying at least five times a day and engaging in thought-provoking discussions with Islamic religious leaders whenever the opportunity arises. "Education and moving with the times is very crucial and vital to the survival of any religion," she stated.

Mrs. Ahmad had been praying all along while her husband was in the ICU. However, she remembers very well how she felt that morning when the Imam had called to say it would be hours before he could make it to the hospital. She doesn't know why, but all thoughts vanished at that very instant. Her mind became still. She felt an unusual sense of calm within. Not only did her body feel lighter, but she also felt a warm surge of energy lifting her up. She had never experienced this before. She was in this state of mind when she saw Father Joe walking toward her.

And at that very moment, she recognized that she had entered into a place where boundaries didn't exist between religions. She was in a spiritual zone.

Was it the fear of losing her husband that ultimately drove her to seek out Father Joe, or was it the power of her conscious and subconscious mind, focused so positively on the recovery of her husband that led him to her? Was it her focused thinking or meditation that ultimately pushed her into the spiritual zone?

I do not have any answers to these questions, but fostering respect and understanding of religions other than our own is a powerful therapy for the cancer that is so aggressively spreading in this world. I recall the now-famous words of Rodney King, the man whose vicious beating by members of the Los Angeles police department was caught on video. Mr. King cried out, "Why can't we all just get along?"

Leaders of world religions should be asking, "Why can't we get along? Why can't we live in a world of religions without borders?"

14. FALL SEVEN TIMES, GET UP EIGHT

*Just because a man lacks the use of his eyes
doesn't mean he lacks vision.*
—Stevie Wonder

*It doesn't matter how you get knocked down in life...
All that matters is that you got to get up.*
—Ben Affleck at the Oscars, 2013

S andy woke up at her usual time, four in the morning. It was still dark and bitter cold outside her three-bedroom ranch located on the south-east corner of her five-acre farm. The ground was covered with two feet of snow. She turned on the radio. The outside temperature was minus ten degrees Fahrenheit, and the forecast for the day called for more snow. It didn't bother her.

She had been born and raised in Wisconsin sixty years ago and by now was used to its harsh winters. She got out of bed, spent thirty minutes in the bathroom, had a simple breakfast of ready-made cereal with milk, and then proceeded outside toward the barn to attend to her dogs. She had been breeding and raising Samoyeds for the past thirty years. Her dogs had won many national championship awards and were fiercely sought after. She had shipped them to many countries around the world and was very proud of that. She loved to stay in touch with their new owners.

Sandy was particularly happy today. A new litter of six had been delivered the day before. The dogs were now waiting for her in the barn. The cold didn't bother them either. In fact, it is never too cold for this breed of dogs, which originated in Siberia.

She filled up the feed trays and poured buckets of warm water for the dogs to drink before it froze. While the dogs were busy eating, she swept the barn floor and checked on the new arrivals. They all looked healthy.

Next, she collected three dozen organic eggs from her free-range chickens from the coop, laid them in egg trays, and loaded them into her truck. Then it was time for her to drive some forty miles for her weekly clinic appointment. It usually took her one hour to cover the distance, but when there was a lot of snow on the road, it could take up to two hours. The snow-removal trucks usually didn't make it to the rural roads until very late in the morning.

She parked her truck in the handicapped parking slot, opened her door, and pressed a button to lower a ramp until it reached the ground. Then, she maneuvered her motorized wheelchair onto the ramp and slowly got herself down to the ground. She used a hand-held remote access to restack the ramp, removed her handbag and the three dozen eggs she had brought for the nurses, and drove her wheelchair into the hospital building. It had started to snow again, exactly as predicted.

Sandy had been diagnosed with MS when she was in her twenties. The disease had progressed until fifteen years ago, when she became totally wheelchair bound. Her arms were strong and she could still transfer herself in and out of the wheelchair. The spasticity and spasms in her legs had become unbearable, but she refused to take more oral drugs because it decreased her concentration. MS had not affected her mind, and she was not going to let the drugs do it either.

Her mind, her thinking, was what kept her going. It allowed her to express herself and do the things she enjoyed doing. Fortunately, the intra-thecal baclofen pump, a device implanted underneath the skin that delivers antispastic medication directly into the spinal canal, has worked very well for her. Gradually, her bladder had stopped responding to various medications, necessitating a major surgery to divert the flow of urine from both the kidneys into an external pouch, which needed to be emptied manually several times a day.

Sandy's bowels had also stopped working. This caused a serious problem, which required another major surgery for a permanent colostomy. This allowed stools to be collected in an external bag. It now takes her at least thirty minutes a day in the bathroom to take care of both the bladder and bowel pouches.

Having failed to respond to conventional MS therapies, Sandy was now receiving a weekly plasmapheresis procedure, a therapy that aims to remove all abnormal antibodies from circulation. MS is believed to be an autoimmune disease. Abnormal antibody production causes destruction of nerve fibers in the brain and spinal cord. The plasmapheresis procedure takes about two hours, during which all of Sandy's blood circulates through a machine about five times, removing the offending antibodies. She has been receiving these therapies now for the past ten years; they appear to have stopped the progression of her disease.

As I walked into the examination room, Sandy was sitting in her wheelchair, which was all decked up with Christmas decorations. The thick white sweatshirt she was wearing had a big sticker of Santa on a sleigh pasted on it with ornate glittery silver snowflakes all over the front and back. This was her artistic creation. Christmas was two weeks away. She had already baked some two hundred cookies as gifts for her neighbors.

For Halloween, she goes all out decorating her chair with scary stuff, including an artificial cobweb. She reached into her handbag and pulled out a Christmas ornament for me. She had also made ornaments for all the staff in my office. The Christmas before last, she had made cards with real dried leaves she had gathered from her huge yard. They sold out within a very short time.

"Sandy, when do you find time to do all this?" I asked.

She smiled and said, "Doc, there is always time if you really want to do anything. I do not like when people talk about not having enough time as an excuse for not doing what they want to do."

Now, when I need to accomplish something or feel too lazy to get up early in the morning to go to the gym, I think about Sandy. I picture her getting up at four in the morning in the dead of winter and heading to the barn to do her chores, and I feel energized. If she can do it, surely I can do whatever I need to do!

I have never seen Sandy look sad or feel sorry for herself. She had no time for that. I once asked her when she had felt the saddest. I thought she would say when she received the diagnosis of MS or when she could no longer walk or when she lost complete control of her bowels and bladder. It took me a while to truly comprehend the answer I received.

"It was when my father passed away. I was nineteen then. He was so young when he died."

For Sandy, it is all about life.

To have a chronic and a debilitating disease, yet wanting very much to lead a life filled with joy and happiness, one has to know and understand people like Sandy. Such people are unfazed by defeat. To give up is never a choice. Confronted by a bad situation, they perceive it as a challenge and just try harder. They notice and acknowledge everything around them; they experience the wonders of nature. They are alive.

To such people, there is a lot more to focus on than their diseases. They live and enjoy every second of every minute. This behavior is just the opposite of those who are unhappy and weighed down by their illnesses. Most of these patients wait for a major event to occur that would somehow profoundly change their status. They wait for a miracle to occur. They look for happiness on the outside, rather than inside themselves. Unlike Sandy, they do not find beauty and purpose in the fallen leaves.

However, this doesn't mean that Sandy is not looking for a miracle or a major breakthrough that would cure her MS. She agreed to receive plasmapheresis, a therapy that was quite controversial at the time, in the hopes that it would help her. But she didn't stop living as she started this therapy. She did not want to miss out on what else her life had to offer until the positive effects of this therapy became evident.

People like Sandy do not put life on hold. They immerse themselves in constructive, purposeful, and joyful activities. They are resilient. A human being is the product of an amazing interaction between the genes inherited from one's parents (genetics) and all the modifications that one's lifestyle imposes on those genes (epigenetics).

* * * * *

The science behind epigenetics would argue that we can influence our genes. Martin Seligman, the father of positive psychology, theorizes that while 60 percent of happiness is determined by our genetics and environment, the remaining 40 percent is up to us. What this means is that behavioral modification over time can have a profound effect on one's state of mind and mood.

Neuroscientist Richard Davidson, professor of psychology and psychiatry at the University of Wisconsin–Madison and founder and chair of the Center for Investigating Healthy Minds, was named one of the one hundred most influential people in the world by *Time* magazine in 2006. He has spent more than forty years studying the human brain and emotion. The conclusion he has reached after all that research is that you can change the brain circuits that govern your emotions and thus shape your emotional style. While we cannot cure patients of their chronic diseases, we can certainly help them to learn how to positively cope with them and lead lives full of joy and happiness.

The emerging field of psychoneuroimmunology (PNI) is the study of the interaction between psychological processes and the nervous and immune systems of the human body. There is now sufficient data to conclude that immune modulation by psychosocial stressors and/or interventions can produce actual changes in health. Just as stressors can produce profound health consequences, alleviating stress has an equally significant positive effect, mediated through the immune and other physiological systems.

Stress is thought to affect immune function through emotional and/or behavioral manifestations such as anxiety, fear, tension, anger, and sadness, as well as physiological changes such as heart rate, blood pressure, and sweating. Researchers have suggested that these changes are beneficial if they are of limited duration, but when stress is chronic, the system is unable to maintain equilibrium or homeostasis, which may then have deleterious effects on the individual's health and well-being.

Mind-body medicine is developing unconventional methods for coping with stress-related disorders. This discipline of medicine has been shown to reduce stress and enhance health. Mind-body techniques help change the way individuals think about the problem, which gives them more control over their responses to stress. Over time, this can influence their genes.

Studying the effects of meditation on quelling the effects of stress on immune and other physiological systems is a growing subfield of neurological research. Modern scientific techniques and instruments, such as functional MRI and electroencephalogram, have been used to see what happens in the body of people when they meditate and how their bodies and brain change after meditating regularly. The early results from these well-designed studies are extremely positive.

Meditation alone has been shown to have a profound effect, not only in the brain but in all of the bodily functions. Could this be the non-pharmacological approach to helping patients with chronic and debilitating diseases? Can it make a difference? While we have no definite answers, my experience related to a person who became a monk for two years and spent most of his time meditating, is very telling.

* * * * *

I recently visited Thailand, where 94 percent of the population practices Buddhism. Traditionally, a Thai male is expected to become a monk for a short period in his life, optimally between the time he finishes school and the time he starts a career or marries. Three months is more usual, although some choose to remain monks for the rest of their lives. A family earns great merit when one of its sons "takes robe and bowl."

There are over 32,000 monasteries in Thailand. The young boys who live in them learn to live simply—no electronic gadgets, no designer clothes, often no shoes—wearing only saffron-colored robes. They walk around the town early in the morning to receive foods from the local people. They are taught to lead well-disciplined spiritual lives. They spend at least four hours a day meditating.

The current King of Thailand, Bhumibol Adulyadej, is the world's longest-serving current head of state and the longest-reigning monarch in Thai history. He too entered a fifteen-day monkhood at age twenty-nine. He stayed at a monastery and followed all the monastic rules before returning to his wife, who had been appointed as his regent during his period of seclusion.

The first place we visited in Bangkok was the magnificent Temple of Golden Buddha. Located in the Chinatown area, this temple is home to the 700-year-old, world's largest solid Buddha image. It is three meters, or close to ten feet, tall and weighs 5.5 tons. It was a plain stucco Buddha image when discovered in 1955. Twenty years later, it was accidently cracked and revealed the precious material inside.

On our way to the temple early in the morning, we passed by a few monks carrying bowls in their hands. They all seemed to be in their teens. Our guide, Srivika, told us how it is customary in Thailand for male teenagers to be ordained as temporary monks. Curious about this practice, I inquired whether it helps them to shape their lives in any way.

Srivika smiled and said, "I think it does. It brings about not only bodily, but spiritual transformation, as well. I know it did for my husband, Viroj!"

Viroj had never become a monk. After seventeen years of marriage and with the consent and full support of his wife, he became a Thai forest monk for two years. Forest monks dwell in the remote wilderness, which supports an atmosphere of renunciation. They mindfully and quietly do their chores or engage in sitting or walking meditation. Their teachers are noted for their creativity in overcoming the hindrances and defilements of the mind. Forest monks are considered to be meditation specialists and work extremely hard to achieve enlightenment.

Viroj observed all of the rules set by the forest monastery. With the shedding of his clothes, he also let go of his family and friends. He shaved his head and donned a simple, saffron colored robe. He learned to avoid thinking about earthly pleasures, and in the mornings, he would go barefoot to receive food for the day from lay people. No telephones, no radio or TV, no Internet, no newspapers, and no fancy treats. He spent most of the two years meditating and in self-realization. Srivika showed me a photo of her husband when he was a monk. He, along with four others, was walking barefoot with his bowls.

"So he had to go out begging for food?" I asked.

Srivika became quiet for a short time, looked into my eyes, and then said to me very softly, "Monks do not beg. They give us a chance to give, so that we can better ourselves. They suffer in the hopes that they can help us attain salvation. If food is not offered, they will fast for the day, but they do not beg for food."

Her words reminded me of two great political giants of our times, Mahatma Gandhi and Sir Winston Churchill. Each led his respective country through its darkest hours to light. They affected the lives of millions of people around the world, and they both shaped the history of the twentieth century. Gandhi and Churchill were totally opposite and different in every aspect, except one: They both agreed on the importance of giving.

Viroj leading his fellow monks with their bowls
for their morning rounds.

My Thai guide Srivika and
her husband Viroj in
Thailand when he was a
monk for two years
(May 2010-June 2012).

The author offering gifts to a Buddhist monk in Thailand.

The monks provide opportunities for people of all ages to give.

"We make a living by what we get, and we make a life by what we give," is what Winston Churchill had to say on the subject.

According to Mahatma Gandhi, "Generosity consists not in the sum given, but the manner in which it is bestowed."

"Viroj came back to me a different person! The two years of monkhood made a world of a difference in him. Before, he was very short-tempered; now he is much calmer, and his communication skills have improved. He is eating better, is exercising more, and is much healthier. He used to have frequent colds but has not had even one since he returned about two years ago."

Srivika continued. "I have noticed a big change in his outlook on life. He used to be very critical of me if I gave anything to charity or money to beggars. I was pleasantly shocked when in the first week after he returned home, he handed out a bag full of fruits to an old man who had approached our car with his hands extended. He now supports my efforts towards charity and recognizes the importance of giving. He is a happier person now, and most important, we have become very close to each other."

* * * * *

Viroj's transformation supports the theory put forth by Martin Seligman and the results of research conducted by Richard Davidson. If two years of meditation can have a lasting effect on emotions and behavior as it did in Viroj, then a daily practice would definitely help patients who feel completely dejected by their disabilities.

In a study published by Dr. Davidson, he measured brain electrical activity before and immediately after and then four months after an eight-week training program in mindfulness meditation. Twenty-five subjects were tested in the meditation group. A wait-list control group (N = 16) was tested at the same points in time as the meditators.

At the end of the eight-week period, subjects in both groups were vaccinated with influenza vaccine. Davidson reported a significant increase in left-sided brain electrical activity, a pattern previously associated with a positive effect in the meditators, compared with the non-meditators. Dr. Davidson was also able to demonstrate that their immune systems were working robustly because the antibody levels to influenza vaccine in blood showed a significant increase in subjects in the meditation group, compared with those in the wait-list control group. These findings lend support to the growing body of research showing that mindfulness meditation produces demonstrable effects on brain and immune function.

* * * * *

Sandy is an exceptional person. She is one of those who are perhaps genetically wired to stay positive in the face of severe calamities. There is an old saying in Japanese, "Fall Seven Times, and Get up Eight." Sandy keeps getting up!

People like Sandy face setbacks, just as everyone else does. The key is that these people don't give up; they keep on going. They see challenges as opportunities, not as problems designed to set them back.

Sandy keeps herself occupied. To her, life and time are way too precious to waste. When I have patients who are giving up due to problems far less serious than Sandy's, I talk to them about her. If possible, I get them to meet with her, and sometimes this does make a difference. Her kindness, energy, and optimistic attitude attract others to her.

So what makes Sandy respond so positively despite her significant disability? To understand this, I sat down with her to ask about her background.

Sandy grew up in a suburb of Milwaukee surrounded by cornfields and hayfields. She loved horses as a child, and when she was a teenager, rather than spending weekends with her friends, she would walk some four miles to a stable to watch horses being ridden in the arena. Even harsh winters could not keep her away from the stables. Walking in the bitter cold would sometimes cause blisters in her feet, but the joy of being with horses was far more important to her than the temporary pain in her feet.

Her father offered to get her a horse, but by then, she had set her eyes on a magnificent Arabian stallion her father couldn't afford. She not only loved horses, but she knew them well. To her, there was no equal to an Arabian.

Historical figures like Genghis Khan, Napoleon, Alexander the Great, and George Washington rode Arabians. It is said that the Prophet Mohammad had proclaimed that Allah had created the Arabian, and that those who treated the horse well would be rewarded in the afterlife.

After graduating from high school, Sandy got a job in Chicago. With the money saved, she bought her first horse, a tall roan-colored Arabian with white socks on its legs. She called him Batal. She purchased many more horses over the years, but Batal was her first love. He went on to win many national championships. By that time, Sandy was becoming well known around the country for her horses.

She married a man who loved and owned horses and lived on a five-acre farm in rural Wisconsin. It was a dream come true for her but, unfortunately, not for long. Soon after they had their only child, a son, she was diagnosed with MS. Her husband withdrew from her, but they stayed married. She needed the health insurance his work provided. Besides, the farm was ideal for her and her horses.

As time passed and she became more disabled, her husband became even more distant and verbally abusive towards her. There were times when he would see her fall down in the barn, but not bother to get up from his chair to help her. She would have to crawl on the filthy floor to get to her wheelchair and struggle herself into it. There were many instances like that.

Sandy, just a few years after her marriage, riding her Arabian horse.

Sandy made costumes for herself and for the horses. They were in great demand and she could not make enough of them!

Her marriage of forty-seven years ended when her husband died not too long ago after suffering miserably from throat and mouth cancer. When I asked Sandy if she had any regrets, she said without any hesitation that she should have divorced her husband a long time ago. After saying this, she was silent for a while, and then she looked at me. Her eyes were moist. Mine were, too.

"You know, Doctor, maybe in a special way he was good for me. The more he said I should not do something because of my MS, the more I challenged myself. I am the type of person who doesn't like to be told what I can and cannot do. The more he stayed away from me, the more resilient I became. I learned to be independent. I focused on the positive. I did not let him affect me. He contributed to my mental and physical independence."

She went on. "There came a time when I could not handle horses anymore, so I started raising dogs. In fact, it was easy doing that from a wheelchair! My hands were so strong that I started to make fancy riding costumes, which sold for over $25,000 apiece. There was great demand for them; I could not make enough of them. A lot has been thrown at me in my life, but I just threw it right back! I believe when life gives you lemons, you should make lemonade and enjoy it with your friends."

Sandy is now in her seventies and continues to remain wheelchair-bound and independent. She drives herself to the clinic for her plasmapheresis therapy and continues to live on her farm.

She had a special gift for me this holiday season. It was wrapped up in fancy paper, tied with homemade multicolored ribbons and had a big bow on the top. The nurses had all gathered around to watch me open the gift. As I tore open the ribbons and the paper, I saw a framed picture of Sandy sitting in her motorized wheelchair with the most beautiful Samoyed dog standing next to her. She looked very happy. She waited a moment and then said,

"Doc, read the trophy I am holding."

Sandy's dog had won a national championship. She had named him, Kumar Khatri! I didn't know what to say. I was speechless. With tears in my eyes, I knelt down and gave her a big hug for teaching me so much over the years.

No matter how bad you think your life is, wake up each day
and be thankful for what you have.
Someone somewhere is fighting just to survive.
—Author Unknown

Sandy with national
champion Samoyed
"Kumar Khatri."

"To give up is not the way I
choose to live with MS"

At age 72, Sandy is still very independent. She is confined to a wheelchair, but continues to drive her van and is able to get in and out with a motorized lift.

Sandy loves to celebrate. She decorates her chair differently for each seasons and holiday.

Here, she's showing off her Christmas decorations.

15. CAREGIVERS

Being unwanted, unloved, uncared for, forgotten by everybody,
I think that is a much greater hunger, a much greater poverty
than the person who has nothing to eat.
—Mother Teresa

One person caring about another
represents life's greatest value.
—Jim Rohn

What would it take to care for Gretchen, a seventy-four-year-old woman with these limitations: She cannot walk or feed herself, needs help with transfers between wheelchair and bed, and has to be turned periodically to prevent pressure sores? She also requires medication six times a day, bathing and dressing, visits to doctors at least once a month, and passive exercises administered to her arms and legs. Gretchen is mentally alert and has the same feelings, aspirations, and needs as able-bodied people do.

What kind of a person does it take to lovingly care for someone like Gretchen? What toll does it take on a person who has been doing this every day for the past twenty years? How do Gretchen and others in similar situations feel about their caregivers?

To understand this special relationship, I talked to Gretchen and her husband, Mendrow, and to my other patients and their caregivers whom I have had the privilege of knowing and caring for over the last forty years.

It was the end of fall and just before the arrival of harsh winter in Wisconsin, when Mendrow brought

Gretchen and Mendrow in their motor home in 2006, leaving their mark in Alaska.

Gretchen to my office for a routine medical check-up. They would soon hit the road to spend the winter in the warmer states, traveling in their motor home. They had been doing this for the past thirty years and both loved it. By the time they return home each year, they would have covered more than six thousand miles. Gretchen is the only quadriplegic I know who does so much traveling in a motor home. Their trip to Alaska covered 10,400 miles! Gretchen is now seventy-four; Mendrow is seventy-five.

Gretchen was thirty-seven when she began to have problems with walking and was diagnosed with a progressive form of MS. Within fifteen years, she was severely disabled and confined to a wheelchair. She could not even feed herself. Mendrow recalls very vividly the vows he had taken fifty-three years ago in a small chapel in a rural town in Wisconsin. He would take care of Gretchen "in sickness and in health, until death do us part." He did not think twice before he slipped into the role of Gretchen's caregiver. He retired from his job a few years later to be with her full time. He has fed her three times a day for the past twenty years. He scratches her face when she has an itch. He knows how irritating it is to her when there are creases in the bed sheets, so he makes sure every night that there are none when he lays her down in bed. He knows to keep her feet uncovered while she is in bed, just the way she likes it.

According to Gretchen, "Anyone with some training can take care of a quadriplegic, but it takes a special person and unconditional love to attend to small things that can make life so much better for a paralyzed person. Such a caregiver can make a person with a disability come alive and want to live again. Mendrow does all this for me without my asking. He knows when to reach out for Kleenex when I have to blow my nose. He knows when I am tired, and he lays me down. I would have to suffer in silence if Mendrow were not there. I would drive my caregiver crazy if I had to request everything Mendrow does for me."

Two years ago, Mendrow suffered a stroke, and Gretchen had to be taken care of by a paid agency for a year as he recuperated. During that year, she developed her first pressure sore, which eventually needed extensive plastic surgery to heal and essentially confined her to bed for several months.

"I was miserable and helpless. It felt like darts were being thrown at me, and I had no strength to move to avoid them. I would lie in my stools for hours until the aide would finally get to me. They were always busy taking care of other patients in the facility. The time without Mendrow was hell for me. I had no complaints about the food they served me. It was good with many options to choose from, but it didn't taste good. There is something about food being offered with love rather than just shoved at you. Plain oatmeal from Mendrow tastes much sweeter and satisfying than the pudding they gave me at the facility."

Mendrow has now recovered and is back to taking care of Gretchen full time. Gretchen is doing much better. The pressure sore has healed, and they will be traveling once again in their motor home to spend the winters in warm southern states. Gretchen was tearful when she told me how fortunate she is to have

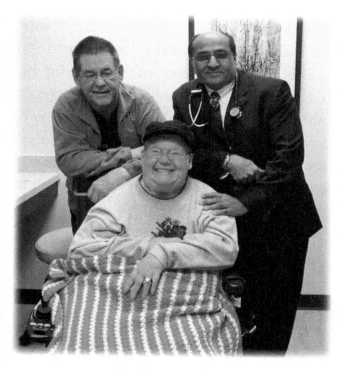

Mendrow and Gretchen with the author in 2014.
They were married in 1960, she was diagnosed with MS in 1977, and has been wheelchair-bound and totally disabled since 1993.

Mendrow. Without him, she would have been dead a long time ago, if not physically, then emotionally for sure. She has no words to describe her love and gratitude for her husband, except to say, "He is my angel."

What about Mendrow? Respectful of his marriage vows, he did commit himself, but deep down does he feel he was served a bad deal? Does he feel resentful? Does he feel like walking away from the role he has assumed? I asked him.

"I never even once thought about leaving Gretchen," he replies. "Sure, there were times when I would get frustrated and tell her that I was leaving and then walk away to another room in the house for a while. But soon the power of my love for her would overcome my frustrations, and I'd return to her. Somehow, those verbal and, at times, nonverbal confrontations helped us to grow in our relationship with each other. We tell each other what we find irritating or upsetting. We have a conversation about what made us upset and then try to find solutions to avoid similar situations in the future."

* * * * *

I would also like to share a story of John, my patient who is severely disabled by MS and is being cared for by his aging parents. Concerned about his increasing disability due to progressive MS, I offered to have a social worker talk to John's parents, now in their late eighties, to find a suitable nursing home for him.

"No, we do not want John to be in a nursing home. He will continue to stay with us, and we can take care of him," insisted his 85-year-old father who, for the past several years, has wheeled his son to the clinic for his intravenous infusion therapy. "No matter how fancy a nursing home, John would not get the care we give him."

I have to agree with him. During a recent short stay at a sub-acute facility after his hospitalization for a severe urinary-tract infection, John was not once sat up in his wheelchair. In the four weeks he stayed there, the food tray would be placed before him three

John with his parents, Howard (85 years old) and Dolores (84 years old), with the author (May, 2014).

times a day and taken away after an hour, but no one took time to coax him to eat in order to get stronger. His parents took him home earlier than recommended by the discharge planners. They gradually nursed him back to his baseline. John was smiling once again. What will happen to John when his parents are no longer able to take care of him?

* * * * *

About twelve years ago, my brother-in-law, Dilsukh, had below-the-knee amputation due to vascular complications related to diabetes. My sister, Hansa, who had been the primary breadwinner for the family, had just retired after having worked for forty-five years. Her eldest daughter was happily married, and Hansa now had a grandson who was her joy. Her son had graduated from a university and landed a good job not too far away from the traditional brick row house they had bought in West London, some forty years ago. Her youngest daughter had found a job and immigrated to the United States. The mortgage on the house was paid in full.

Major renovations a few years ago to accommodate Hansa's disabled mother-in-law had increased the value of their house. In addition to working full time, Hansa had been the caregiver for her mother-in-law for several years before she died at home, just the way she wanted to.

My sister was now looking forward to enjoying her golden years when the sudden turn in events changed everything. While he was in the hospital recuperating from the leg amputation, Dilsukh went into serious congestive heart failure. His condition was further compromised by renal failure, which had to be managed diligently with diet and medications to avoid renal dialysis. This would not be difficult unless the patient also suffers from a long history of bipolar disorder, which had been diagnosed only recently.

Bipolar was not well controlled by the limited medications Dilsukh could take because of his other medical issues. Rather than placing him in a nursing home, as was suggested by the doctors, Hansa brought him home. She became his primary caregiver and gradually nursed him back to a reasonable state of health.

Whenever I visit London, I stay with them, and Hansa has also brought Dilsukh to our home in Milwaukee a few times. I have observed closely what it takes to be a caregiver for a disabled person who doesn't take care of himself. Despite being a diabetic, my brother-in-law would secretly eat food he should not, refuses to exercise, and slings hurtful words at my sister, on whom he is dependent for all his activities of daily living.

Why does she still continue to be his caregiver? Why did she recently undertake a major trip to a rural town in India to fulfill his wish for a pilgrimage to a temple that houses their family deity?

Getting around and traveling with a disabled person in the United Kingdom or the United States is difficult, but it is a lot worse in India, where the infrastructure to accommodate the disabled is severely lacking. Nevertheless, Hansa managed, and she was very happy and proud of the fact that she could do it for him. Why? She, too, has diabetes and back problems, which require frequent epidural injections. These give her relief until she reinjures her back by lifting her husband or moving the wheelchair in and out of the car. However, more than the physical pain, it is the loneliness of being a spouse who has been forced through circumstances to be a caregiver, rather than simply a spouse, that hurts her most of all.

Caregiving is very physical and structured. Caregivers go through the routine of completing the tasks for the day, and then repeat the whole process the next day and the next and the next. There is no time to address their own emotional needs or of those they are taking care of. Everything becomes mechanical, and this takes a heavy toll on the caregivers. They feel "alone," even when they are not.

I was in London three years ago to celebrate Hansa and Dilsukh's fiftieth wedding anniversary. This joyous occasion was attended by more than three hundred friends and family members, some of whom we had not seen for many years. After a great dinner, when the band started to play, everyone stopped talking and focused their eyes on Hansa and Dilsukh. Normally, they would all get on the dance floor and have fun, but now, seeing Dilsukh in a wheelchair, they didn't know how to react.

Hansa & Disukh celebrating their 50th wedding anniversary (2011).

After a few minutes, Hansa wheeled Dilsukh to the center of the floor and started to dance with him, maneuvering the wheelchair to the rhythm of the music. The audience broke into thunderous applause, watched them dance the first song, and then joined them on the floor. Tears ran down Dilsukh's cheeks. Only a few years ago, while he was in the hospital severely ill, he had not wanted to live. With his leg amputated and his other medical problems, he was afraid he would lend up in a nursing home. And to him, he had declared, that would be a slow death.

* * * * *

Richard, a quadriplegic due to MS, was taken care of by his wife for 21 years, until he passed away in 2012. They had been married for eighteen years when he was diagnosed with MS soon after the birth of their third child. Richard was confined to a wheelchair within seven years. For more than two decades, Judy was his caregiver. She fed him, lifted him in and out of the bed, catheterized his bladder four times a day, brushed his teeth, shaved him every day, and changed his position several times a day. She did everything for him, in addition to taking care of the house, the children, and herself. During the time he was paralyzed, he never suffered a pressure sore. When I asked Judy recently what made her do the things she did for Richard, she answered without any hesitation.

"I am not a quitter. It was something I had to do. Quitting the marriage when the going got tough never occurred to me. I am a very physical person, so taking

Judith and Richard were married in 1967. He was diagnosed with MS in 1984, shortly after the birth of their third child.

Richard, with wife Judith and grandson (2011).

Richard passed away in 2012.

care of Richard was not a problem. My father was a homebuilder, and I grew up helping him, from laying the concrete to erecting the walls. It is in my nature to build. Caring for Richard gave me the great satisfaction of building and taking our marriage to another level. We both grew in our marriage, and I truly experienced the 'marriage bliss' they talk about. To me, it was an energy that elevated us far beyond physical and emotional love. Sure, it was tough at times; but as I look back, now that Richard is gone, I feel God placed me in the situation I was in. I would do it all over again!"

Now, as she has time to reflect, Judy feels that she got so much in return from caring for Richard.

"Not only did I grow spiritually, but I came to appreciate the power of mind over body. Richard was a quadriplegic and could not move, but his mind was not trapped in his body. Through his mind, he took me places to which I would not have traveled. He showed me how to live even though you cannot move, how not to despair at small things in life. Every time I fed him, I recognized how fortunate I was. It inspired me to do more to achieve my goals in life. He showed me that nothing is impossible when you put your mind to it. Caring for Richard helped me enrich my soul."

* * * * *

Mendrow, Hansa, and Judy were committed caregivers to their spouses. Quitting was not their way. They all had enormous strength to support their marriage vows; they all felt divine intervention at play, which placed them in a special situation; and they all benefitted from their commitments. Elderly spouses are often enormously loyal to each other, as one slips into the role of being a caregiver without hesitation.

But what about younger couples? How difficult is it when one of them becomes disabled? MS is the commonest cause of disability, after trauma, in young adults in this country. More than two hundred new MS patients are diagnosed each week in the United States, and one every hour elsewhere around the world.

Fifty percent of MS patients develop permanent disability within ten years of diagnosis. Those who need total care are helpless. They are at the mercy of their providers and feel quite vulnerable. I have observed some caregivers verbally declare their frustrations in the presence of the ones they care for. I have seen the eyes of my patients tearing up, but they never respond to the abuse. They simply look away to hide their sadness and pain. Rocking the boat is not in their best interest, they feel, because the alternative could be even worse.

More than food and shelter, the disabled crave love and compassion. They need to feel wanted. There is an Indian saying, "Not wealth, not food, but a little genuine comforting oomph can breathe life into a dead person." Caring and comforting love can heal the soul. It takes unconditional love to offer such comfort and care. According to Judy, couples who have been married for some time perceive love differently. The partners become one over time. They feel the pain of the disabled spouse.

For most parents of disabled children, offering unconditional love comes naturally. The dynamics here are somewhat different. Disabled children actually do feel secure and less vulnerable when they are being cared for by their parents. They stand their ground and do not hesitate to ask for what they need. They know quite well that the spouses can divorce each other, but the parent-child relationship is different. Unless the parents themselves become disabled, they usually continue to take care of their disabled children at home.

With married couples, it takes special people like Mendrow, Hansa, and Judy to do what they do. There is no reward or medal; the satisfaction of being able to care for their loved ones is their highest award. Recognizing that their spouses are not replaceable, that they are human beings with feelings, becomes the driving force and gives them strength to continue.

"Life has its ups and downs. No one knows what the future holds for anyone. At the end of the day and at the end of your life you should be able to say that you did the right thing!" according to Hansa. "I hope I am also educating my children in the process to never give up! It is important that they learn how to treat their loved ones with dignity. The ultimate judge of character is the way you treat a person when he or she is totally helpless."

It is love coupled by inherent human nature to be kind that stirs the conscience of a family member to be a caregiver. This theory is supported by a study sponsored by EUROFAMCARE, Services for Supporting Family Carers of Elderly People in Europe, which revealed that 57 percent of people listed affection as their primary motivator, while only 28 percent chose a sense of duty or a personal sense of obligation as theirs. Very few people attributed their motivation to having no alternative but to accept the role. Doing the "right thing" seemed to be the guiding force for many of the caregivers I interviewed. Collectively, they had served more than three hundred years as caregivers.

* * * * *

Richard and Roberta were twenty-three and twenty-one when they got married. Roberta had been diagnosed with MS at age twenty. She delivered her daughter at age twenty-three and a few months later, became permanently confined to a wheelchair. Their daughter is now a young woman and living on her own. They have been married for thirty-one years.

Richard became Roberta's caregiver within three years of their marriage. He gets up every day at 4:00 a.m., gives Roberta a shower and dresses her, gets her breakfast, and settles her in a motorized wheelchair. By 5:00 a.m., he leaves home for work. He returns home at three, takes her to the bathroom, washes her up, and gets dinner ready. They eat dinner by six and then have some quality time before

Richard & Roberta in 2014. Married at 21, Roberta became wheelchair bound within three years of their marriage, soon after the birth of their daughter. They have been married for 31 years.

it is time to go to sleep. The next day the cycle continues.

Richard has been spending more time caring for Roberta than in the past, due to her worsening disability. She was able to physically take care and help raise her daughter even when she was in a wheelchair, but now she has to rely on Richard for almost everything.

"My co-workers, friends, and even my own siblings ask me why I don't just walk away. It is difficult and, at times, very rough to juggle work and life at home. What they see is a lot of physical hard work and the time taken away from other pleasures in life. What they do not see is how caring for Roberta has made me grow up spiritually.

"My upbringing as a child was not the best. My mother passed away on Mother's Day when I was eleven. My father took to alcohol quite heavily and became a very difficult person to be around. I could not wait to leave the house and be on my own. He was never a role model for me, but indirectly, he helped to shape me. I tried not to be like him, and in fact, I became just the opposite of him. Religion was not a part of my life growing up, but I do recognize that being with Roberta, being in love with her, and caring for her is what religion would have wanted me to do. To be human is to care for others.

"When I was a teenager, I would have made fun of someone in a wheelchair. Knowing Roberta has taught me what it takes physically and emotionally to be in a wheelchair—the toll it takes on her psyche. Yet, she tries to stay positive because no one wants to be around a person when she is in a depressed mood. Surely, I would not have married Roberta had I known what the future was going to be like, but once I fell in love with her, it did not matter anymore. I married her despite her diagnosis of MS. I cannot imagine my life without her. We are committed to each other until we cross the finish line.

"In some ways, I feel I have left my friends and family members way behind. I cannot talk about my frustrations and my stress to them because they really do not comprehend the real reason why I do what I do. Sure, caring for Roberta has taken me away from things I enjoy doing. I can't bicycle too far away from home in case there is an emergency and I have to return home quickly. I know that Roberta will be dying to get off that chair and eagerly awaits my arrival at home every afternoon at 3:00. There are times when I do verbally express my frustrations and walk away from her for a short time. Then, I see her face and those beautiful captivating eyes, and she draws me to her. I cannot stay away from her for too long."

Roberta was listening to all that Richard was telling me. Quite a few times, while he talked, she cried.

Her tears were not the tears of sadness or of sorrow, but rather of appreciation and of knowing that, despite being disabled and not able to assume the traditional responsibilities in the marriage, she was loved and wanted, unconditionally.

"Knowing that Richard still loves me and wants to be with me keeps me going. It lightens up the burden I bear. It helps me to get up in the morning," says Roberta.

Richard is, however, very concerned that if Roberta continues to worsen, he may have to cut his hours at work or even be forced to quit work so that he can provide the help she would need. Getting private agencies to help would be unaffordable in the long run.

* * * * *

The financial burden of caring can be extremely stressful. As of 2012, fifty-two million caregivers provide care to adults with disabilities in this country. The majority (83 percent) are family caregivers, of whom 90 percent are unpaid. The value of unpaid family caregivers will likely continue to be the largest source of long-term care services in the United States. The over-sixty-five population will more than double between the years 2000 and 2030, increasing from 35.1 million to 71.5 million. According to the

American Association of Retired Persons (AARP) Public Policy Institute, caregiver services were valued at $450 billion per year in 2009, up from $375 billion in year 2007. As time goes by, the burden of caregiving will fall on family members, who are also growing older and experiencing health problems. Eventually, this will require paid agencies to provide the care for both populations.

The economic impact of caregiving will be considerable as Baby Boomers age. The Alzheimer's Association of America projects that by 2050, the number of patients will triple to fifteen million, which will considerably increase the burden of unpaid care. Caregivers receive no compensation for caring for their family members. Because most don't have the financial resources to hire outside help, their choices are limited: either quit working or put their loved ones in nursing homes.

The other significant and growing problem is related to the caregivers themselves. They tend to suffer physically and emotionally. They do not see a doctor because they put their families' needs first (67 percent report that is a major reason). More than half (51 percent) say they do not have time to take care of themselves, and almost half (49 percent) admit that they are too tired to do so (National Alliance for Caregiving, 2004). Caregivers are also more prone to depression, physical ailments, and social isolation. They need psychological and emotional support, as well as time off periodically to prevent burnout.

Caregivers quite often choke-up when I genuinely acknowledge their enormous dedication and commitments towards their loved ones. Unless you live with someone who is totally or partially disabled 24/7, it is extremely difficult to fathom what is required to take care of that person.

The toll on marriages can be serious. According to data released in 2012 by the National Center for Health Statistics, 43 percent of first marriages end in separation or divorce within fifteen years; 20 percent end within five years. While some studies show the divorce rate for couples with MS (and chronic illness in general) slightly elevated, many others show rates surprisingly near the same as (if not a little lower than) the general population.

According to Dr. Rosalind Kalb, in her book, *Multiple Sclerosis: A Guide for Families*, the divorce rate may be a bit lower for people with MS than the general population because of fear of being alone with the illness, a sense of commitment or obligation, and the need to maintain insurance coverage for the person with MS.

The gender of the partner who is ill makes a huge difference in the rates of divorce. The divorce rate for marriages in which the husband had MS was as low as 3 percent, while nearly 21 percent of couples in which the wife had MS, ended in divorce. This is a significant finding, since women are more often afflicted with the disease than men (four to one). Early signs of burnout include neglecting one's self, alcohol abuse, low threshold for losing one's temper, and insomnia. If these signs are recognized early, appropriate interventions can prevent many problems, such as divorce or serious illness.

* * * * *

My sister, Hansa, knows all too well the medical consequences of stress. "I have to allocate some time during the day for myself to zone out, to be alone. Sometimes, this is not possible depending on how Dilsukh is doing. But for the most part, I hire people from an agency, so that I can step out for a short time to recharge myself." The way Hansa tries to deal with stress is to walk away when Dilsukh is in a bad mood. "Staying positive is what keeps me going. I look at the glass as half full. It is not easy at times, but I have gotten better at it.

"Before I took the trip to India with Dilsukh, I pictured in my mind exactly how it was going to be, from the time we would leave the house in London up to our return home. I visualized everything—all the details—and entertained only positive thoughts. Never did I imagine anything bad would happen. Then, I put my faith in God and took the trip. It was amazing; all went well, just as I had planned.

"He had always wanted to make that trip, but after he became disabled, he didn't speak about it because he knew it would never happen. To make it happen for him and to see the joy on his face was priceless. What I received from that experience was also priceless. To check off such a dream on your personal bucket list is an accomplishment, but to help a disabled person check it off of his or her list is an indescribable gift." I continue to learn from Hansa and all of my patients.

A month after I had finished writing this story, Dilsukh passed away peacefully. He woke up early that day, had a shower and a shave, put on fresh clothes; and then, as he settled in his bed, he asked Hansa to sit next to him and hold his hand. He kept looking at her, and every time she tried to get up, he would insist that she stay a little longer. An hour later, he complained of chest pain and had some difficulty breathing. She quickly called the paramedics, but recognizing that he was behaving as though his end was near, she summoned her son and Dilsukh's younger brother to be with him.

By the time they arrived, Dilsukh's breathing had become very shallow and labored. His younger brother asked him if had anything he would like to say.

Dilsukh smiled a little. As he kept his eyes on Hansa and held her hand, he said, "I am happy and content. Hansa is with me, and she is holding my hand. I do not wish for anything else."

A few minutes later he passed away with his eyes still open and fixed on Hansa. These final moments, even though painful for Hansa, were just as important to her as when they were first married. Knowing that she had done the best she could in caring for Dilsukh and that her efforts had made a huge difference in his life meant a lot to her. Her marriage had its ups and down, but her unconditional love for Dilsukh and the sacrifices she had made at the expense of her own health to care for him were rewarded in the final moments of his life when all he wanted was to be held by Hansa. To her, that was the ultimate expression of his love for her. That moment and that experience washed away all the bad memories she had of her marriage. It more than validated all she had done for so long.

* * * * *

Caregiving takes a significant physical and emotional toll on the givers. In certain instances, it expedites the aging process. I have noticed it firsthand. But caregivers gain much in return, both spiritually and emotionally, in being able to end their life journeys on a positive note. As Richard Niesing had said, "... and when you cross the finish line, you know in your heart that you have done the right thing."

Many years ago, on the fifteenth day of his fast to stop the Hindu-Muslim riots soon after India and Pakistan achieved their independence from Britain, Mahatma Gandhi was approached by a Hindu man. The man confessed to killing a Muslim boy and said that he would go to hell for the crime he had committed.

Gandhi, who was by now very frail and weak, looked at him and whispered, "There is a way out. Go find an orphaned Muslim boy, and adopt him as your own. Just make sure that you raise him as a Muslim." According to Gandhi, adoption was the highest form of unconditional love.

I believe that caring for a disabled person is also the highest form of unconditional love one can offer to a fellow human being.

The best and most beautiful things in the world
cannot be seen or even touched.
They must be felt with the heart.
—Helen Keller

16. PRACTICING MEDICINE IN THE DIGITAL AGE

I'm sorry, it's true. Having children really changes your view on these things. We're born, we live for a brief instant, and we die. It's been happening for a long time. Technology is not changing it much — if at all.
—Steve Jobs

A physician is an unfortunate gentleman who is every day required to perform a miracle; namely to reconcile health with intemperance."
—François Marie Arouet Voltaire

If migraine patients have a common and legitimate second complaint besides their migraines, it is that they have not been listened to by physicians. Looked at, investigated, drugged, charged, but not listened to.
—Oliver Sacks

My nephew was waiting for me at the San Antonio airport to whisk me to the hospital to be at the bedside of my brother-in-law, Hasmukh. He had been hospitalized a few days earlier because of severe bleeding in his gut, which had since taken a turn for the worse. He was in a coma and required a mechanical breathing machine to keep him alive. At age seventy-five, with significant other medical problems (including obesity, which had gotten out of control because of chronic steroid usage for renal disease; diabetes; hypertension; and chronic drug-dependent depression), his prognosis looked quite grim.

My sister and their daughter, who is a family practice physician, were sitting by his bedside when I entered his room. They both looked exhausted, having spent most of the last four days in the hospital with Hasmukh. He looked peaceful. The only movements were those of his chest, heaving up and down due to air being pushed rhythmically into it by a respirator. I glanced at the monitor by his bedside. His vital signs and blood oxygenation numbers looked good. A catheter was draining clear urine from his bladder into a bag hanging from the side of his bed.

I turned to him to do a brief neurological examination. As a neurologist, I have examined many patients in similar conditions. As I pulled off his blanket, I noticed that his right arm was swollen. I looked at his daughter, who immediately told me that she had mentioned it to the doctor who, after a quick glance at the arm, had brushed it off as being superficial thrombosis, which warranted no further tests or therapy.

Since Hasmukh was heavily sedated with medications, I could not assess his neurological status, but we were both very concerned about the swelling in his arm. At her insistence, an ultrasound of his arm was reluctantly ordered. Unfortunately, this revealed a serious problem. The intravenous line that was inserted into his forearm a few days ago had caused a significant thrombosis leading up to a major blood vessel in his chest, with the potential for causing a clot in his lungs.

A specialist was called in. He recommended that blood-thinning medicine be started immediately, with the understanding that Hasmukh could bleed again in his gut. Failing to start the medication involved the considerable risk of a pulmonary embolus, which would surely kill him.

The next few days were critical, and we hardly left him alone. It bothered me that the doctor, who could rattle off to me in great detail all the laboratory results, had not bothered to examine his patient even when his daughter, who is also a physician, raised a concern. To him, the computer readouts had been all normal, and he saw no indication that anything out of the ordinary was happening.

To enter Hasmukh's room, I had to pass by the doctor's work station, where I observed that, despite having the twenty-bed ICU filled with very sick patients, he spent a lot of time on the computer. This worried me but did not surprise me. Since the hospital had adopted electronic health records (EHRs), the doctors had no choice but to spend a considerable amount of time on computers to stay in compliance. The $20 billion Health Information Technology for Economic and Clinical Health (HITECH) Act of 2009 represented the largest U.S. initiative to encourage the widespread use of EHR. Within a very short time, the law changed the way doctors practice medicine in this country.

At my own hospital-based clinic in Milwaukee, we had our mandatory introduction to EHR in October 2011. The hospital wanted to take advantage of the financial incentives offered, but the window of opportunity was very short. Under the federal guidelines, those who did not adopt EHR in a meaningful way by 2014 faced a significant financial penalty. The arrival of EHR at our clinic put an end to paper charts and dictations related to patients' visits, which were later transcribed into legible notes.

Within days of its implementation, it became obvious to all of us that the system would also bring an end to the way we interacted with our patients. It would significantly slow the flow of patients and, as a result, decrease revenue to our clinic.

This proved to be true not only with our practice, but also at other centers throughout the country. It is becoming a national trend. Newly released data in 2014 from the marketing and research firm, MPI Group and Medical Economics, suggest that 79 percent of one thousand doctors surveyed had very negative opinions of EHR. They felt implementation of EHR in their offices was not worth the cost, and the majority of respondents said their EHR systems result in financial losses. The findings of the two-year study presented in 2013 are further corroborated by the findings of a January 2013 RAND Corporation study, detailed in *Health Affairs*, the *New York Times*, and *USA Today*.

"Poor EHR usability, time-consuming data entry, interference with face-to-face patient care, inefficient and less-fulfilling work content, inability to exchange health information between EHR products, and degradation of clinical documentation were prominent sources of professional dissatisfaction," the report says.

Healthcare providers are now forced to bring computers into examination rooms and type in the patient's symptoms and physical findings, order all the necessary tests and treatment plans, and complete all of this in less than forty-five minutes for a new patient and in less than twenty minutes for a follow-up visit.

Something had to give for this "meaningful use of EHR"—a term coined by lawmakers in Washington, DC—to succeed. What gave, sad to say, was the soul of physicians who no longer knew the color of their patients' eyes because they didn't have time to look.

To make enough money to pay for office overhead, medical malpractice insurance, student loans, decent salaries, and a small amount of savings each year, a doctor has to see at least twenty-five patients a day, both new and follow-up. This is a tremendous burden on healthcare providers, and as a result, the quality of care suffers. Doctors no longer have the time to bond with their patients or their families. Numerous study results also document that introduction of EHR leads to decreased numbers of patients seen in a day, which in turn translates to falling revenues.

Another outcome is that healthcare providers devote more time to doing "clerical work" than spending quality time with their patients. In the MPI Group and Medical Economics study, one of the surveyed physicians summed up the problem this way: "We used to see thirty-two patients a day with one tech, and now we struggle to see twenty-four patients a day with four techs. And we provide worse care!"

The HITECH Act ushered in by Congress is forcing the healers of America to practice medicine guided by digital intelligence. In the examination room, the computer is now getting more attention than the patient.

* * * * *

N ot too long ago, I was asked to see an 80-year-old woman who had been hospitalized because of severe pain in her left leg. An MRI of her hip and knee joints showed arthritic changes. A young orthopedic doctor determined that, based on the MRI, the pain was obviously due to the knee problem. To him, this explained very well why she could not stand and walk.

Despite a steroid injection in the knee, her pain worsened; I was called in for a consultation. Within a few minutes of conversation with the patient, it became very clear that she had been walking independently without any problems until two days before her hospitalization. This would make a diagnosis of chronic arthritis as the cause of her painful left leg an unlikely cause of her problem.

I pulled off the blanket to examine the leg. The pain she described was present in the lower part of her abdomen, hip, and down to the knee. She winced and let out a cry as I gently palpated the left lower abdominal area. She had been on chronic blood-thinning medicine because of an irregular heart rate. My diagnosis that bleeding in the retroperitoneal area (where nerves that exit the spinal cord run through a space between the abdomen and back) was causing her to have severe pain was confirmed by a CT scan.

This is an easy diagnosis to make, even by a physician in training, as long as someone listens to and examines the patient. When I looked at her EHR, there were voluminous notes recorded by healthcare providers, including her history of a tonsillectomy when she was a child, all stating that her abdominal examination was "negative"!

Doctors are pressured to "capture" everything on the EHR because payments are directly linked to how detailed the charting of the examination is. In this patient, if the smoking history had been omitted and not checked in the correct box, a financial penalty would have had to be paid.

What the system is forcing doctors to do is to miss the forest for the trees. This problem is widespread and growing. I have spoken to many doctors, and their responses are unanimous: "EHR is destroying the patient-doctor relationship. It is not *what* you prescribe, but *how* you prescribe that is important in healing the patient. The human connection is central to diagnosing the basic cause of what ails the patient."

An illustration from a recent article by Elizabeth Toll, M.D., in the *Journal of the American Medical Association* (JAMA, 2012), shown opposite, portrays a gut-wrenching picture drawn by a seven-year-old-girl, depicting her recent visit to her doctor. It shows her on the examining table, her older sister seated nearby in a chair, and her mother cradling her baby sister. The doctor sat staring at the computer, his back to the patient and everyone else! If a seven-year-old can get it, why is it taking so long for legislators in Washington to get it?

A projected savings of $77 billion annually for a 90 percent EHR adoption rate would be dwarfed by the tremendous loss of the true healers of America. What is more frightening is that this loss would be irreparable. The art of medicine is developed over years by seeing and caring for hundreds of patients. How can you capture this experience and translate it into a

If a seven-year-old patient can tell the story with a picture she drew, there is something drastically wrong the way we practice medicine. I just hope it is not too late to change.

language that is understood by a computer? EHR is good at storing all the test results and patient demographics, so multiple physicians caring for the patient can have a ready access to these records. It can also keep up with advancing medical technologies, but it has yet to learn how to emotionally connect with a patient. The practice of digital medicine cannot teach or direct a physician how to hold the hand of a patient who has just lost his or her spouse of fifty years. My colleagues have stated so elegantly, "It takes a lot more than prescribing drugs to heal a patient."

* * * * *

It was Hasmukh's fifth day in the ICU. In the three days I had been present in the room, from morning until evening, I never saw the ICU doctor touch, let alone examine, him. His care was based on whatever information that doctor was receiving via the computer. It concerned me enough to ask for a face-to-face meeting with the ICU doctor.

I was impressed by what he knew about Hasmukh's urine output and fluid balance, his laboratory results, and of all the medications he was receiving. However, I was very much troubled by the fact that he showed no emotion. It was as though I was interacting with a robot. His demeanor was strictly "business." It became very obvious that he was at the meeting because he was asked to be there, not because he wanted to come. None of us in the family felt any connection with him. He exuded no warmth whatsoever.

Now, this experience is not unique to our family. In hospital- or clinic-driven surveys to capture patient satisfaction, the major complaint is that patients spend very little time with their doctors. Clinic visits are rushed. Patients are asking why their doctors no longer make any eye contact with them. Doctors are busy with their computers. They no longer have (or take) time to talk about how the family is doing or whether their patient is under any stress. The system now in place is such that doctors cannot do any of that, even if they want to. For a personal bond to develop between a doctor and a patient, it takes time and commitment on both their parts.

The ICU doctor for my brother-in-law was spending a lot of time with the computer, which told him all he needed to know about Hasmukh. The computer had become a surrogate for his patient. He had bonded with the surrogate. Perhaps that is why he had no emotional feelings towards us.

Several scientific studies support the significant therapeutic value of a healthy relationship between doctor and patient. In a controlled study of placebo versus a real antidepressant drug in depressed patients, a good relationship turned out to be more powerful in promoting recovery from depression than whether the patient received an active treatment or placebo. Especially powerful is how the patient feels about the doctor. This observation holds true for other medical conditions as well.

If doctors are no longer able to deliver medicine without this "powerful healing energy" (also called the "positive concern"), billions of dollars will be lost because it will take patients a very long time to recover, if they recover at all. Most important, quality of care will suffer. The main objective of EHR is to improve quality of care, not to erode it.

Change is good. Change leads to progress. The medical field has seen and embraced remarkable scientific advances over the years to improve quality of life and prolong survival. The driving force behind almost all medical advances has been the sage, old saying, "Necessity is the mother of invention."

On the other hand, pushing an agenda before its time can lead to disastrous outcomes. Legislators need to stop playing doctors. The United States leads the world in medical innovation. Most recent medical breakthroughs have occurred in this country. We have the best and brightest practicing medicine in state-of-the-art facilities. Patients come from all over the world to have access to the latest medical technologies and innovations. This unprecedented progress has occurred despite any agenda set by legislators.

Contrary to the common myth, studies have shown that physicians—especially older ones—are not technophobes or dinosaurs. They adapt to technology very quickly and readily if it improves patient care. When the technology is right and the need is there, an appropriate digital device will be invented to foster and preserve the physician-patient relationship. For now, resources should be directed toward studying what makes this "doctor-patient" relationship so vital to the healing process.

With EHR, we are experimenting with an unproven, yet mandatory, technology at a national level. No other industry has ever been under a universal mandate to adopt a new technology before its effects are fully studied. Congress keeps coming up with schemes to try to control healthcare costs. Establishing financial incentives for electronic health records (EHRs) appears to be just one more example of where Congress has again fallen short, based on this report of physician outcry over EHR functionality and costs.

In the long run, mandatory EHR implementation may prove to be costly. If early results are correct and predictive, it could well lead to the demise of the centuries-old art that heals. This is a real concern. I experienced it first hand when I was in the ICU with my brother-in-law.

Hasmukh had gradually improved. He no longer needed the support of a respirator. The breathing tube that was in his trachea was pulled out. He could talk a little, but his breathing did not appear normal to me. It was labored and shallow, and he could barely cough. This was even more concerning when he tried to swallow liquids, and the fluid went down the wrong way. He had no strength to cough, and we had to suction it out manually.

The ICU doctor walked in an hour after the tube was removed and ordered Hasmukh to be discharged from the ICU to a regular room. When I expressed my concern about his breathing and requested him to let him stay in the ICU another day, it fell on deaf ears.

"His numbers all look OK, and there is absolutely no justification for him to stay in the ICU," I was informed by his doctor.

I have cared for many patients in similar situations before, and I knew very well that, even though his numbers looked good at that moment, they may not a few hours later. The doctor had not examined him or seen how he coughed when the liquid diet he had ordered went down the wrong way. He was guided by what he saw on his computer.

I was quite upset at this turn of events when a senior cardiologist walked into the room to examine

Hasmukh. He talked to him, his wife, and his daughter and expressed his happiness now that Hasmukh was off the respirator. He then proceeded to examine him. Using a stethoscope, he listened to Hasmukh's heart and then his lungs from front and back. Finally, he pulled the stethoscope from his ears and looked at me. The smile on his face a few seconds ago was now replaced by a grim look.

"His lungs are wet. Unfortunately, he will have to stay a couple of extra days in the ICU so that we can remove the extra fluid from his circulation."

Then he gave a big reassuring smile as he held Hasmukh's hand in his and said, "You will be fine. We just want to make sure you do not have to come back to the ICU!"

Over the next twenty-four hours, removal of three liters of fluid from Hasmukh's blood circulatory system brought about significant relief and comfort. There was an immediate improvement in his breathing and speech, and he could swallow much better.

* * * * *

The cardiologist who had predicted a serious problem if he were not treated right away belongs to the "old school," which despite federal pressure to change, continues to place the patient first, before the computer. Many others give up and have chosen to take premature retirement. There is no study or data available to state exactly how serious this problem may be, but I do know of a handful of doctors who have left the profession because of this issue. Many more continue to complain and will eventually give up practicing medicine.

The American Academy of Neurology's Workforce Task Force reported its findings in 2013. The current demand for neurologist services already exceeds the supply, and by 2025, it is projected to worsen, exacerbating already long wait times and reducing access to care for Medicaid beneficiaries. At present, reimbursement for caring for a Medicaid patient for a forty-five minute consultation is, for the most part, far less than what it costs to cover even office overhead expenses! This is bound to get worse if the system is not corrected. It may lead to untold and perhaps irreparable damage.

With digital-age medicine, it is the next generation of healers about whom we should be concerned. They will no longer know what it means to put their finger on the pulse.

There is a growing concern in the medical community about the regulations being imposed by those in Congress and other agencies, which put financial gains before patient care. These people may not be standing in our exam rooms, but their influence is highly palpable. Politicians tell physicians what software to use in their offices, which EHR options must be utilized during an office visit, and how they will be penalized if they do not follow mandated guidelines. A vise already put around the neck of physicians is being slowly tightened and will eventually choke the life out of the patient-physician relationship.

Physicians, regardless of their ages, have consistently embraced technology for its opportunities to improve efficiency and the quality of care they provide to their patients. Once celebrated as the next big thing in the healthcare world, EHR has a long way to go in terms of physician satisfaction, according to survey data from American EHR Partners released in March 2013 by the Healthcare Information and Management Systems Society (HIMSS). The study, based on 4,279 responses to multiple surveys of clinicians conducted between March 2010 and December 2012, revealed that physician disillusionment with EHR systems is growing rapidly. With two years of experience with this mandate, more than one-third of physicians would not recommend their EHR system to a colleague, are very dissatisfied with their EHR system's usability, and have not yet returned to pre-EHR implementation productivity levels.

The government's intention to improve overall quality and cost of healthcare with EHR implementation is also being questioned by physicians who have already adopted this system.

In 2005, a RAND Corporation report predicted that widespread use of EHR could save the US healthcare system $81 billion per year. Although the use of EHR has increased steadily, a new RAND analysis finds those earlier predictions overly optimistic. There is no denying that forced reduction of "face-to face" interaction between patient and physician severely compromises care. This leads to increased health risks, clinical mistakes, poor outcomes, and soaring health bills.

However, EHR has been a boon to hospitals. In a fee-for-service payment system, EHR makes sure no procedures are overlooked. Every encounter, every procedure, is now captured and billed. Cutting, pasting, and importing already populated information about various multiple medical issues the patient may have or ever had with a click of a button, allows for a higher billing for a physician without improving quality of care to patients.

Before EHR, hospital administrators constantly reminded doctors to record as many medical conditions as possible in order to improve reimbursement. Recently, while looking up EHR for laboratory results I had ordered for a patient hospitalized for less than forty-eight hours, I counted at least thirty blood-glucose reports (finger-stick tests that diabetic patients routinely do on their own at home but are now performed by nurses at the hospital). Undoubtedly, these were captured by the sophisticated billing programs attached to EHR.

There is no doubt that EHR has been of tremendous help when it comes to reviewing all test results and medications. Physicians can access them remotely, order tests, and change medications while they are thousands of miles away from the patient.

What EHR fails miserably to accomplish is what is at the heart of patient care: connecting the patient to the physician. We physicians ought to have a say in how we care for our patients. We have been doing this for centuries. Medical care costs are rising in this country not because of the absence of external mandates imposed on doctors. Mandatory guidelines handed down to doctors not only increase the cost, but also lower the standard of care. This is what the new and emerging surveys tell us.

Managed care has its own agenda as well. It makes money by reducing the fees it pays to doctors, while asking them to do the same amount of work, or more, for less money. Doctors have little data and less expertise in these negotiations and have consistently come out badly. The uneven playing field on which doctors find themselves these days—having to deal with hospital administrators, mandatory EHR guidelines, and managed care—makes collective bargaining seem attractive. Collective bargaining should give doctors power to negotiate wages, benefits, and working conditions. But doctors are barred by federal anti-trust laws from bargaining collectively. Government, managed healthcare, hospital administrators, and lawyers all take advantage of this fact to impose their will on the very profession that heals America.

The dynamics of the healthcare environment are changing rapidly, and so is the practice of medicine. Today's medical students will care for tomorrow's patients. To ensure and to preserve the medical excellence for which this country has been recognized, progress needs to continue and changes need to be made, but not at the expense of what we have already achieved and learned over the years.

17. BRAIN DEAD

Some things scratch the surface while others strike at your soul.
—Gianna Perad

The pain was unbearable. After several epidural steroid injections and two failed back surgeries, Corey had come to rely heavily on narcotics for temporary relief from pain.

Taking a few steps to the bathroom, even with the aid of a walker, was now excruciatingly painful. This is no way to live, he thought. At forty, he felt like a burden to his wife of sixteen years, Kimberly. He had not worked for the last three of those years after his fall off a ladder while at work.

A major surgery to fix two fractured lumbar vertebrae did not help relieve his pain or improve the strength in his legs. He could not walk and was required to take strong pain pills to give him partial relief. He had been confined to a wheelchair ever since his third and last back surgery, a year ago.

Corey was tired and depressed. He couldn't remember when he had last slept well. Maybe a few hours of good, deep sleep would help him escape from his pain for a short while, he thought. He took a handful of sleeping pills, half a bottle of Tylenol, and several Vicodin tablets, washing it all down with six cans of beer. He was hoping his pain would stop, even for a short while. He turned on the television, lay down on his bed, and waited for the pills and the liquor to kick in. He closed his eyes; within a few minutes, he passed out.

"We have a young man in his late thirties, overdosed on Tylenol and a bunch of other drugs," a paramedic radioed to the trauma center at a major hospital about three miles away. "He is comatose and barely breathing. I can't feel his pulse very well. He is going down fast!"

While one of the paramedics inserted a tube down Corey's trachea to deliver air with a hand-operated ambu bag, the other successfully secured an intravenous line and started to pump fluids into Corey's bloodstream.

"We are coming in!" one of the paramedics announced, giving a heads-up to the triage nurse at the trauma center. A team of doctors, nurses, and technicians were waiting for Corey at the other end.

According to the National Institute of Mental Health, suicide is the tenth leading cause of death in this country; in young adults, it is third on the list. An acute Tylenol overdose kills more people each year than any other drug. The emergency room (ER) team of doctors was well prepared to deal with such situations. As soon as the ambulance came to a halt, the back doors were flung open, and within a few seconds, Corey was whisked into a special emergency room. He was immediately connected to a respirator, and the entire team of medical staff swung into action.

One of the doctors inserted a triple lumen catheter into the subclavian vein in his right upper chest to make it easier and faster to simultaneously administer different medications. The radial artery at his wrist was catheterized to allow his blood pressure to be monitored continuously and for the nurses to draw blood without having to repeatedly puncture him.

Corey's clothes were cut open and stripped off. Leads were applied to his chest to monitor his heart, a catheter was inserted into his penis to collect and measure his urine output, and a tube was inserted into his stomach.

Once the tube's position was verified by an x-ray, activated charcoal was pumped into his stomach to absorb any drugs that might still be present. The main ingredient in Tylenol (acetaminophen) is metabolized into N-acetyl-p-benzoquinoneimine (NAPQI), which rapidly depletes the liver's natural antioxidant (glutathione) and directly damages liver cells.

Acetaminophen, which is found in over a hundred different drugs, has been cited by the American

Association of Poison Control Centers as the leading cause of liver failure in the United States. An antidote called acetylcysteine is very effective in preventing liver failure, but it has to be administered within six hours of an overdose.

The cascade of toxic events in the liver had already begun in Corey, as evidenced by the reports of blood tests that were sent to the computer screen directly from the laboratory. Not only his liver but also his kidneys were severely damaged by the Tylenol and alcohol overdose. He had not put out any urine since arriving in the ER.

As soon as his vital signs stabilized, Corey was moved to the surgical intensive care unit, where another team of doctors, who were specialists in organ transplants, awaited him. Corey would most likely die if he didn't get a liver transplant as soon as possible.

According to the United Organ Sharing Network Organization in the U.S., liver failure as a result of acetaminophen toxicity is the second most common reason for liver transplant.

The multidisciplinary medical team went into action. Based on his medical condition and the fact that he had no prior history of liver problems, Corey was given the preferred high-priority status to receive a transplant. A report was sent out to all of the organ procurement centers in the Midwest, alerting them of an immediate need of a liver.

By the following morning, the news arrived that a liver was available. The family of a young girl, who had died in an automobile accident in Illinois, had willed her organs for transplantation. Corey's family was relieved to hear the news, but was also pained by the fact that some parents in Illinois had lost a daughter early that morning. Corey was now being prepared for the liver transplant.

As I powered down my computer and picked up my briefcase to go home early that afternoon, my pager went off. I was asked to see a young man *STAT* (a medical term meaning "immediately") in the ICU. Apparently Corey had experienced a cardiac arrest and had been without a heartbeat for up to five minutes before doctors were able to get his heart started again. I was asked to evaluate him and to make a recommendation as to whether the surgeons should proceed with the liver transplant or call it off because the patient was possibly brain dead.

A donor organ is a precious commodity. More than twenty thousand people are on the waiting list for liver transplants alone in this country. Perhaps there was someone out there who would benefit from this liver more than Corey. The helicopter was ready to take off with the harvested liver from a hospital in Rockford, Illinois, but was asked to wait until I had seen and evaluated the patient. I called the ICU nurse, told her that I was on my way and would be there in fifteen minutes, and ordered an emergent electroencephalogram (EEG), a test that would record the electrical activity from Corey's brain.

Before I entered his room, I saw Corey's young wife Kimberly waiting outside. Our eyes locked. She knew exactly why a neurologist had been called in to see her husband. I didn't talk to her at that time, but her eyes told me a lot. She had been in a state of shock ever since she had found her husband unconscious when she returned home from working third shift. Much had transpired since the paramedics had picked him up from their house the day before, and she was still in her work clothes. She had not left her husband's side except to go to the bathroom.

The news that a liver was now available and that it would be transplanted into Corey within a few hours had lifted her hopes. But now she was worried. The cardiac arrest and the considerable time it had taken to resuscitate him may have caused irreversible brain damage and, according to the surgeon who explained the situation to her, this could disqualify him for the transplant. Besides, one needed to consider the total cost of the transplant, which might run over half a million dollars. If Corey was declared brain dead by a neurologist, the liver could be diverted to someone else who could really benefit from it.

Caring for a drug-overdose case is never easy, but it is even harder to deal with those who are left behind. They are the ones who are hit hard and suffer not only from the loss of their loved ones, but also because of the emotional guilt trip they go through. The question they constantly battle with is: Could they have prevented the tragedy?

Physicians are programmed to prolong life at whatever cost. However, they are for the most part not adequately prepared to deal with the consequences of their actions. The feelings of loved ones are often overlooked or ignored, not necessarily out of arrogance but rather because of ignorance. Physicians are trained to heal the body, but not the soul.

As more technological advances are made, we are certain to find that computers are becoming the interface between patients and doctors or that doctors will act more like computers. The doctors are already focusing more time on computers than on their patients.

As I stepped into the room, Kimberly and I continued to look at each other until I turned my head toward her husband. The EEG technician shook her head slightly to indicate that, to her, the brain electrical activity didn't look good. I proceeded with my neurological examination, which took about fifteen minutes to complete.

None of the clinical signs I tried to elicit indicated any hope for Corey. He was comatose and did not respond to painful stimuli. Turning his head from side

to side did not evoke any eye movements, corneal re-
flexes were absent, his pupils were not reactive to
light, and he did not breathe on his own when I took
him off the ventilator for a few moments.

I asked myself, "Does Corey meet all the criteria
for 'brain dead'?" I turned to the EEG technician, who
turned the computer screen toward me so I could review the EEG tracings. After a quick glance at the
screen, my heart sank. The brain electrical activity
looked flat, which could mean that the brain had
suffered irreversibly due to lack of oxygen during the
cardiac arrest, and there was no hope for him. I
looked at the 30-minute recording but didn't see any
electrical brain activity. I asked the technician to
increase the sensitivity of the recording, and we now
began to see some very small, slow waves randomly
appearing on the screen. She shook her head again,
and I knew what she was thinking.

What should I recommend to the surgeon?
Clinically, I had not observed any signs of Corey's
brain being "alive," and the EGG, except for the occasional small waves, looked flat. It was not only a
tough decision to make, but an impossible one,
inasmuch as he had come to this state after an overdose of drugs and alcohol.

I blocked out all other thoughts from my mind and
focused solely on Corey. If he did not receive the
transplant, he would surely die. This was certain. If

he did get the liver, could he survive; and, if he did, what would be the quality of his life? If he was truly "brain dead" or close to it, would the rest of his life on this earth be in a vegetative state? Should I wait until the drugs and alcohol were out of his system and re-examine him? Surely, by that time, the available organ would have been transplanted into someone else.

Once again, I looked at the EEG tracings on the computer screen. They didn't look any different. And then I saw Kimberly's face reflected on the screen. She was standing behind me but not too far away from the recording machine. It was then that I made up my mind. I called the surgeons and told them to get ready for the transplant.

The ICU nurse who was taking care of Corey looked at me in bewilderment. Was I thinking correctly? Was I sure of my decision? They knew very well that it was likely that Corey was brain dead, and they were simply hoping to get a confirmation from me. They couldn't believe what I had just done. I looked at them for a while, nodded my head, and moved towards Kimberly to tell her of my decision.

Tears rolled down her cheeks; she held my hand in both of hers and spoke volumes, though not in words.

Neither the surgeon nor I slept much that night. Corey had taken a turn for the worse after the transplant. His blood pressure had dropped, and he had generalized seizures, requiring medications for both conditions. Thankfully, an emergency CT scan of his brain did not reveal any bleeding in the brain, which can occur in the setting of severe liver failure.

I had an early-morning flight to catch the next day to deliver a lecture in Atlanta in the evening. My associate would take over Corey's care. It was Friday; I returned to Milwaukee late on Sunday evening. Early Monday morning, I went to the hospital and walked straight to the ICU. I had not obtained any updates on Corey while I was away, but I was anxious to see what had happened to him.

Over the years, I have been surprised at how intensely I could get involved, both intellectually and emotionally, with my patients while I am at work. When I am away, I seem to block out those feelings—not completely, but enough to allow me to live my life. And yet, as soon as I am at work again, it all comes back with the same intensity of involvement and caring as before.

I was almost there. My heart had started to race a little. Would I find the bed empty or perhaps occupied by a new patient? I picked up my pace, walked into the room, and as I pulled the curtains to the side, I froze at what I saw! Corey was sitting on the edge of his bed, eating breakfast!

I had goose bumps all over me. I was speechless. I didn't know what to say to him. All sorts of thoughts started to race in my mind. I knew very well that he had been "brain dead" when I had recommended the transplant to proceed.

What had happened? Why was he alive? What made me say "yes" to the transplant? There was no scientific basis to my decision, and yet, I had said yes. Why? Then I remembered seeing the reflection of his wife's face on the computer screen and how something in me had stirred up an intense feeling of hope for her husband.

I cannot exactly find the words to describe that feeling, but her eyes had conveyed something powerful. I had made my decision, based neither on what I had learned in medical school nor on any scientific findings, but rather on a strangely positive energy that I had perceived around Corey and his wife. There is no scientific way to recognize or measure that feeling.

One gradually begins to learn to appreciate that sixth sense from patients and their families. One learns by being with them and by listening to them, and more importantly, by reading their eyes. I have heard from other physicians that, from time to time, they have had similar experiences around seriously ill patients.

Physicians quite often excel in keeping death away, but sadly, they may fail to nurture the soul that is so vital to keeping the body "alive." We may lose this art forever as we begin to place computers before the patient. This federally regulated and mandated practice of recording everything on computers by healthcare providers is encouraged by hospitals which want to take advantage of the financial incentives offered. Under the federal guidelines, those who do not adopt electronic health records (EHR) in a meaningful way by 2014, also face a significant financial penalty.

* * * * *

Corey made a great recovery and was discharged from the hospital in less than two weeks. He was doing well when I called him a few weeks later to ask him if he would come to my office to have his photo taken. I was so moved by his recovery that I wanted to share his story as a teaching lesson to younger physicians in training. I wanted to impress on them that sometimes, you have to listen to your heart when making tough decisions. You do not have to go by the book or science every time. I wanted to tell them, "Let us not act like computers when it comes to healing the sick."

Corey readily agreed to come to my office, and he and Kimberly arrived promptly at the appointed time. He was dressed in a brown business suit and a tie. He looked well. We had our photos taken together and chatted for a while. Then, I thanked both of them for finding the time for my request and giving me the consent to use his photo for teaching purposes.

As I started to walk towards my office, Corey called out and said he was still confused and wanted to know why I really wanted his photo. There are countless other liver transplant survivors, so why him? His question stopped me in midstride. I turned around and looked at him for a few seconds and then at his wife. She nodded her head slightly. It was true—Corey really didn't know why I had photographed him!

This would take some time, so I led them to a small conference room and asked them to sit down. After I explained the circumstances under which I had authorized the transplant, I could see that Corey

The author with Corey and Kimberly after his recovery (2007).

was visibly shaking, and then, he started to cry uncontrollably. He hugged me and said he had no idea how close he had come to death. He considered his survival from the overdose a miracle, but the realization that his living or dying had been so critically dependent on a single person was shocking to him. It was frightening to me, as well. I still get goose bumps when I think about it.

It has been seven years since Corey was brought to the ER in a comatose state. He is now a successful businessman, has two children, and never misses sending me a thank you note each Christmas. And every year, when I hold his card in my hands, I still ask the same question: What made me say, "yes" to the liver transplant.

We all had considered him to be clinically "brain dead." Sight, hearing, smell, taste, and touch are the tools most of us depend on to perceive the world. Additionally, physicians rely on clinical and laboratory tools to objectively evaluate these functions in a human being. All these conventional tests available to me failed to show that Corey's brain was "alive."

Then why had I said yes to the liver transplant? Was my decision driven by my sixth sense? Was I able to perceive things that were outside the range of the conventional senses, through some other channel for which there is no anatomical or neurological explanation?

Earlier, I mentioned that it was the reflection of Kimberly's face on the EEG monitoring screen that drove me to my decision, but was it really? I had hesitated about my decision even before I saw her image. Was my sixth sense telling me something at that time that made me to pause?

It is not unusual for an experienced physician to declare that a patient "doesn't look right" in the absence of any laboratory or objective clinical findings. I have heard from many physicians who have sent patients to hospitals for just that reason, to find out later that they indeed had serious, often life-threatening, conditions.

Trusting one's "unconscious" brain or sixth sense is very important and should not be excluded when examining a patient. Almost all of experienced nurses who spend long hours with patients can accurately predict if the patient is not doing well based on their sixth sense. Doctors listen and take the nurses very seriously if they receive a call stating that "the patient is just not looking right." The sixth sense is when something stirs in your gut.

Physicians with encyclopedic text-book knowledge of many medical conditions who can rattle off with ease recent scientific literature, sometimes lack common-sense, bed-side healing techniques. Touching patients, looking into their eyes, and listening to them and their caregivers, can provide many more clues to what is ailing the patient than all the investigations you may order or all the theoretical knowledge you may possess.

These hands-on experiences over time are registered in the brain, which allows one to "develop a feeling" when faced with a particular situation. These feelings can be intense, as was the image of Kimberley's face on the EEG screen monitor.

Emotional attachment at any level with a critically ill patient or their loved ones does sometimes invoke a premonitory response in a physician, be it positive or negative. Based on my clinical and physiological evaluations, the most logical recommendation would have been not to proceed with the transplant. However, during that brief period as I meditated and got myself "into the zone," I came up with a decision quite contrary to one I would have reached had I relied solely on objective evidence. Was that my supernatural moment?

I may not get my questions answered, but I can say with some certainty that there are times when you also must trust your subconscious mind to make the decisions. It does not happen often, but all of us, I am sure, have had the experience when something stirs in our gut, a feeling that tells us to act in certain ways which looking back, was the right decision. The power of the sixth sense or of the subconscious mind is complex and can produce results that defy the scientific mind.

FINAL THOUGHTS

There is a Taoist saying: "When the student is ready, the teacher appears."

Writing about my patients, their caregivers and family members, as well as the frustrations faced by countless physicians I have spoken to, has had a profound effect on me. There has been a reawakening in me about the reason I chose to be a physician in the first place. What I was taught by my teachers in medical school and my residency is no longer valid in light of the rapidly changing ways that physicians are required to practice medicine today.

Finding a balance among regulatory requirements, administrative duties, and the third-party payers who dictate "how and what to prescribe," on the one hand, and what is in the best interest of our patients, on the other hand, is an art that must be embraced and taught by every medical school.

Rather than running away or, as the saying goes, "burying one's head in sand," physicians need to fight back. Patients are simply not the number of "cases" we must see in a day or relative value units (RVUs) earned—a method used for calculating the volume of work to financially compensate a physician.

Writing this book has taught me to take my place, to reclaim my worth as a healer, rather than what I have been forced to become. Every case, every RUV, is a patient who is a son, a daughter, a parent, or a spouse. No matter how disabled, each one has aspirations and dreams, even if these desires are only in their imaginations. Each one should be treated with dignity and respect.

Treating my patients, conducting countless interviews, and researching the topics in this book have reinforced in me the far-reaching influence the mind has on healing. Healthcare providers need to play a greater role in invoking the "power of the positive mind" in their patients. We may not always have a medicine or a cure for every disease, but the *oomph* a patient receives from the comforting touch of a physician may just *heal the soul.*

ACKNOWLEDGMENTS

I t would have been impossible to write this book without the many opportunities I have been given and the lessons I have learned during more than thirty years of caring for my patients. I will be forever grateful for the wisdom and guidance of my teachers and my parents who taught me to appreciate all that was offered to me.

I would especially like to recognize Bobbi Linkemer, who did an outstanding job as my editor. She was excellent at getting the best out of me. She asked appropriate questions, made wonderful suggestions, and nudged me ever so slightly if I slacked off, all of which made this a better book.

I want to thank my teacher and mentor, Dr. Michael P. McQuillen, for reviewing all of my stories and using his magic "green ink" to breathe life into them.

I owe a debt of gratitude to my family, Radovan Stojanovich; all my brothers and sisters; my sister-in-law Jagruti; niece, Kajal; my staff at the clinic; my personal trainer, Caleb Dewall, and gym buddy, Nick Schubert—all of whom gladly read the stories and offered not only criticism, but also encouragement and motivation for me to continue.

Many thanks to my publisher, Kira Henschel, for her guidance and calm tolerance of me; Peggy Nehmen for her sensitive cover design; Poonam Suryavanshi and Nishit Nirmal for their excellent marketing skills; to Yogesh Khatri, for his tremendous organizational skills and promotional ideas; Pamela Dry for her superb administrative skills; and anyone else I may have inadvertently omitted, I say *Thank you!*

INDEX

Stories and case histories of individual patients used as examples are found under "patient stories."

— **U** —

— **T** —

ABOUT THE AUTHOR

Bhupendra Odhavji Khatri, MD, is the founding medical director of The Regional MS Center, Center for Neurological Disorders, in Milwaukee, Wisconsin, one of the largest multiple sclerosis centers in the United States.

Born and raised in Kenya, of Indian descent, Dr. Khatri earned his medical degree at The Grant Medical College in Mumbai, India; then, interned and trained in neurology at Sir J. J. Group of Hospitals in Mumbai. He completed his residency in neurology at the Medical College of Wisconsin, where he continued as an associate professor of neurology until 1990, when he opened the Center for Neurological Disorders in Milwaukee.

Dr. Khatri is a pioneer in the field of therapeutic plasmapheresis. His research and participation in clinical trials have led to an effective plasmapheresis protocol therapies for various autoimmune neurological disorders.

Rated by peers as one of the best neurologists in Milwaukee, Dr. Khatri is a frequent lecturer at universities, professional neurological and MS organizations, and insurance and pharmaceutical companies nationally and internationally. He speaks on caring for patients with neurological disorders, as well as the power of positive thinking and the subconscious mind on healing.

Dr. Khatri's numerous original articles have been published in peer-reviewed medical journals, as well as chapters in medical textbooks. In his first book, *Healing the Soul: Unexpected Stories of Courage, Hope, and the Power of Mind*, Dr. Khatri reflects on the art of practicing medicine and the influence a positive attitude can have on patients' medical outcomes.

 Facebook.com/HealingTheSoul

 Group: Healing the Soul Book

 @healingsoulbook

 https://www.youtube.com/HealingtheSoulBook

CPSIA information can be obtained
at www.ICGtesting.com
Printed in the USA
LVOW01s0856030316

477616LV00001B/1/P